Twayne's English Authors Series

SYLVIA E. BOWMAN, *Editor*

INDIANA UNIVERSITY

Abraham Cowley

Abraham Cowley

By JAMES G. TAAFFE
Case Western Reserve University

Twayne Publishers, Inc.   ::   New York

Preface

Since Abraham Cowley's reputation has been overshadowed by that of John Donne and Ben Jonson, readers will find only a few of his poems available in modern anthologies of seventeenth-century poetry. A. R. Waller's standard two-volume edition (1905-1906) of Cowley's English works was issued without critical apparatus (part of which was prepared but never published); the volume containing the major poems, however, is out of print. One is fortunate, therefore, that L. C. Martin's selections (1949) from Cowley remain available. The Latin poems and the Latin drama are almost inaccessible, found together only in a now rare edition brought out by the indefatigable Alexander Grosart in 1881. There are two excellent biographical studies; Arthur Nethercot's *Abraham Cowley: The Muse's Hannibal* (1931) is the standard work; its contemporary, Jean Loiseau's exhaustive *Abraham Cowley: sa Vie, son Oeuvre* (1931), is a valuable supplement. One ought to mention also Samuel Johnson's shorter but acute consideration of Cowley, the first of his *Lives of the English Poets* (1779-81). From the day of Johnson, each time the controversy over the meaning of "metaphysical" resumes, there is some discussion of Cowley and his poetry.

Arthur Nethercot's series of articles, dating from the late 1920's and early 1930's, represents the beginning of modern consideration of Cowley, while the more recent commentary has been by Geoffrey Walton (1955) and David Rawlinson (1963). Robert Hinman's *Abraham Cowley's World of Order* (1960), tracing Cowley's interest in science and the shaping effect of scientific thought on his poetry, deserves separate recognition; it is a definitive analysis of the poet's work from that aspect. To all these studies, of course, I am deeply indebted.

This present book has no major interest in biography, nor has it a theme, such as Hinman's, to trace throughout the poems.

Preface

It is a chronological survey and critical discussion of representative examples from each genre in which Cowley wrote; it is a consideration of how he worked, of his ideas and occupations as they reflect themselves in his work; and of the relationship of his work to that of others (especially Donne) with which it is frequently compared. Often I permit the poems to speak for themselves because I think the reader ought to listen to the poet's voice as much as possible. This book is neither an apology for Cowley nor an essay to revive his work; it attempts to analyze and evaluate his productions so the reader may see what it was that Cowley's own century praised so highly.

A glance through Jean Loiseau's *Abraham Cowley's Reputation in England* (1931) reveals the proof of Cowley's great popularity in his own time. "More famous by his pen than his sword" declared the *Weekly Intelligencer* for April 12, 1655, when it reported the fact of his imprisonment; and John Milton's widow, Elizabeth Minshull Milton, said that Spenser, Shakespeare, and Cowley had been "approved most of our English poets" by her late husband. Many of Cowley's poems were turned into songs—additional proof of their popularity—by William King, Henry Purcell, and Pietro Ruggiero. Nearly a hundred coaches followed in the funeral procession, John Evelyn noted, on that day when the poet was buried in Westminster Abbey next to Chaucer and near Spenser. "Mr. Cowley," said King Charles II, "had not left a better man behind him in England"; and Dryden declared him "the darling of my youth." Cowley remained for many, in Anthony à Wood's phrase, "prince of poets."

These tributes, however, were soon forgotten. By the end of the century Cowley was no longer considered the great voice of his age. From then on his reputation has been in eclipse. While many consider his work an example of the disintegration of the Metaphysical mode, only a few now find something there to praise. To read Cowley's poems now, however, is more than an exercise in literary history. Reading them makes one aware of Cowley's sensitivity to the major (and minor) literary and scientific interests of the seventeenth century. Cowley's works reflect many of his age's preoccupations, and reading them enables one to discover something of the excitement of life in a period of revolution and transition. This book is intended for those who wish to read about Cowley's poetry and prose without engaging in long debate about the characteristics of Metaphysical poetry; it is my hope that they will find something there to praise without the addition of that qualifying argument.

JAMES G. TAAFFE

Case Western Reserve University

Contents

Contents

Chronology

1618   Abraham Cowley born in London; the seventh son of Thomas Cowley, a stationer.

1629   Admitted as King's Scholar to Westminster School.

1633   *Poetical Blossoms.*

1636   Second edition of *Poetical Blossoms,* with *Sylva.* Graduated from Westminster; unsuccessful candidate for Cambridge.

1637   Third edition of *Poetical Blossoms.* Admitted to Trinity College.

1638   *Loves Riddle.* Latin comedy, *Naufragium Joculare,* played at Trinity (February 2).

1639   Bachelor of Arts, Cambridge.

1641   *The Guardian* played for Prince Charles (March 12).

1642   Master of Arts, Cambridge.

1643   Formally dispossessed by the commission of the Earl of Manchester (April 8). *The Puritan and the Papist.* Refuge sought at St. John's College, Oxford.

1646   In Paris, secretary to Lord Jermyn.

1647   *The Mistress.*

1650   *The Guardian.*

1650-
1651   On a secret mission to Jersey.

1654-
1655   Return to England; arrest and imprisonment; release from prison on the bond of Dr. Charles Scarborough.

1656   *Poems* (including "Miscellanies," "The Mistress," "Pindaric Odes," and the "Davideis").

1657   Incorporated as Doctor of Physic (December 2).

1658   Rewrites *The Guardian* as *Cutter of Coleman Street.*

1659-
1660   Return to France (?).

1661   *A Discourse by Way of Vision, Concerning the Government of Oliver Cromwell. A Proposition for the Advancement of Experimental Philosophy.* Performance of *Cutter of Coleman Street* (December 16).

1662   *A Couleii Plantarum Libri Duo* (*A Book of Poems about Plants in Two Sections by Abraham Cowley*).

1663 *Verses lately Written upon Several Occasions*. Publication of *Cutter of Coleman Street*. Retirement to Barn Elms in Kent.

1665 Move to Chertsey.

1667 Death, July 28. Buried in Westminster Abbey.

1668 Posthumous publication of *The Works of Mr. Abraham Cowley*, ed. by Thomas Sprat.

CHAPTER 1

"My childish Muse is in her Spring"

I "Chimes of Verse"

AT fifteen, three years before he was to graduate from West-minster, precocious Abraham Cowley published his first poems, a small quarto of thirty-two leaves entitled *Poetical Blossoms*. When the book was published in 1633, Thomas Sprat, Cowley's biographer and literary executor, wrote that "in the thirteenth year of his age there came forth a little Book under his Name."[1] Robert Vaughan's portrait of Cowley also recorded "Aetatisuae 13. Anno *1633*." Both Sprat and Vaughan, carried away by their enthusiasm, are obviously wrong;[2] but, even for a boy of fifteen, the volume is remarkable.

In the author's preface one is surprised to discover that two of the poems were written before he entered his teens: "I should not bee angrie to see any one burne my *Pyramus*, and *Thisbe*, nay I would doe it my selfe, but that I hope a pardon may easily bee gotten for the errors of ten yeeres age. My *Constantia* and *Philetus* confesseth me two yeeres older when I writ it."[3] These two major poems and three shorter works were preten-tiously accompanied by sets of dedicatory verses and an invoca-tion to Melpomene. Here, however, were "many things that might well become the vigour and force of a manly Wit."[4]

A tragic romance set in exotic Florence, "Constantia and Phile-tus," opens the volume. The narrative concerns a familiar love triangle. Philetus, in love with Constantia, befriends her brother, Philocrates, in order to be near his beloved. To him, he pours out his chaste emotion; and Philocrates arranges an interview for the lovers. Constantia's father, however, hopes to forward a match between his daughter and Guiscardo, who is "base and Poore" of soul but not in worldly riches. Philetus and his lady plan to run off together, having met secretly during one of her father's outings; but Guiscardo follows them, and the de-

13

nouement involves the deaths of the four principals. Caught by
Guiscardo, Philetus is killed; Philocrates and Guiscardo slay one
another; and the good Constantia, who dies by her own hand,
breathes her last over the body of her Philetus. Lacking any
sustained and developed dramatic interest or original character
portrayal, the romance gains most of its appeal from its sympa-
thetic treatment of the lovers' *hereos;* more significantly, it re-
veals Cowley's awareness of several major verse traditions.

Although the narrative source is unknown, Cowley's stanzas
are probably modeled after the Spenserian sestet (*ababcc*); and
his final couplets, like Spenser's, are contained, epigrammatic
units:

> Who leaves to guide the Ship when stormes arise,
> Is guilty both of sinne, and cowardise. (XXXV)

> *Why, he who hath all sorrowes borne before,*
> *Needeth not feare to be opprest with more.* (XL)

> *But there is no Physitian can apply*
> *A medicine, ere he know the Malady.* (XLVI)

> *Hee who acquainteth others with his mone,*
> *Addes to his friends griefe, but not cures his owne.* (XLVII)

> . . . That fire
> Which is kept close, burnes with the greatest ire. (LXII)[5]

The romance also reveals the youthful author's acquaintance
with Renaissance love verses, plays on friendship, the courtly
love tradition, and Petrarchan convention. One may compare,
for instance, these conceits of Cowley's with these in Petrarch's
sonnets XXXII, XCII, and CLXXXII:

> And framing her attractive eyes so bright
> Spent all her wit in studie, that they might
> Keepe th'earth from *Chaos,* and eternall night. (III)

> Her hayre was brighter than the beames which are
> A Crowne to *Phoebus,* and her breath so sweet,
> It did transcend Arabian odours farre,
> Or th'smelling Flowers, wherewith the Spring doth greet
>   Approaching Summer, teeth like falling snow
>   For white, were placed in a double row. (IV)

The mayden Lillyes at her lovely sight
Waxt pale with envie, and from thence grew white. (V)

The glorious beames of her fayre Eyes did move,
And light beholders on their way to Love. (VII)

Aurora blusht at such a sight unknowne,
To see those cheekes were redder then her owne. (X)[6]

Of course, Cowley did not overlook the cliché of love verses, the famous galley image:

Home he retyr'd, his Soule he brought not home,
Just like a Ship whil'st every mounting wave
Tost by enraged *Boreas* up and downe,
Threatens the Mariner with a gaping grave;
   Such did his case, such did his state appeare,
   Alike distracted between hope and feare. (XVIII)[7]

In this passage just quoted, one is reminded of Thomas Wyatt's "My galley charged with forgetfulness" (a translation of Petrarch's CXXXVII), and Spenser's XXXIV, "Lyke as a ship," from the *Amoretti*. The reader is soon aware that Cowley's romance is a grab bag of literary clichés, one complete with the intricate word play of an echo song not often so polished in the verse of a youth of twelve:

Oh! what hath caus'd my killing miseries?
Eyes, Eccho *said, What hath detain'd my ease?*
Ease, straight the resonable Nymph replyes,
That nothing can my troubled minde appease:
   Peace, Eccho *answers. What, is any nigh?*
   Quoth he: at which, she quickly utters, I.

Is't Eccho *answers? tell mee then thy will:*
I will, shee said. What shall I get (quoth he)
By loving still? to which she answers, ill.
Ill? shall I void of wisht for pleasure dye?
   I; shall not I who toyle in ceaselesse paine,
   Some pleasure know? no, she replyes againe.

False and inconstant Nymph, thou lyest (quoth he)
Thou lyest, shee said, And I deserv'd her hate.
If I should thee beleeve; beleeve, (saith shee)
For why thy idle words are of no weight.

> *Weigh it (shee replyes) I therefore will depart.*
> *To which, resounding* Eccho *answers: part.*[8]

For the second poem, the fresh and charming "The Tragicall
Historie of Pyramus *and* Thisbe," Cowley turned to Ovid's
Metamorphoses, a work familiar then to every schoolboy. And,
like every schoolboy, Cowley knew of the translation by Arthur
Golding; his poem, in fact, reveals more Golding than Ovid.[9]
Cowley's Babylonian lovers struggle tragically in the noble
passion:

> Like as a Bird which in a Net is tane
> By strugling more entangles in the ginne;
> So they who in Loves Labyrinth remaine,
> With striving never can a freedome gaine.
>   The way to enter's broad, but being in,
>   No art, no labour, can an *exit* win.   (IV)[10]

Again the final couplets tend to be gnomic and epigrammatic,
and the Petrarchan elaborations are part of Cowley's contribu-
tion to Ovid's version. Like Golding, Cowley provides additional
dimension to Thisbe's character. Ovid's episode moves swiftly
to its denouement, the lovers never doubting each other's de-
votion; but Cowley's Thisbe pauses to sing a lovely song which
reveals her serious concern over Pyramus' delay:

> *Come Love, why stayest thou? The night*
> *Will vanish ere wee taste delight:*
> *The Moone obscures her selfe from sight,*
> *Thou absent, whose eyes give her light.*
>
> *Come quickly, Deare, be briefe as Time.*
> *Or wee by Morne shall be o'retane,*
> *Loves Joy's thine owne as well as mine,*
> *Spend not therefore the time in vaine.*

> Here doubtfull thoughts broke off her pleasant *Song,*
> Against her love for staying shee gan crie;
> Her *Pyramus* shee thought did tarry long,
> And that his absence did her too much wrong.
>   Then betwixt longing hope, and jealousie,
>   Shee feares, yet's loth, to tax his loyaltie.

> Sometimes shee thinkes, that hee hath her forsaken;
> Sometimes, that danger hath befallen to him;

> Shee feares that hee another love hath taken:
> Which being but imagin'd, soone doth waken
>   Numberlesse thoughts, which on her heart doe fling
>   Feares, that her future fate too truely sing.[11]

Her doubts and fears are given lyric emphasis as Cowley's version expands her role, and these interspersed songs are the most attractive sections of the verse romance. They reveal a genuine lyric gift which is obvious in the grace and facility of the concluding epitaph:

> 1.
> *Underneath this Marble Stone,*
> *Lye two Beauties joyn'd in one.*

> 2.
> *Two whose Loves Death could not sever,*
> *For both liv'd, both dy'd together.*

> 3.
> *Two whose soules, being too divine*
> *For earth, in their owne Spheare now shine.*

> 4.
> *Who have left their Loves to Fame,*
> *And their earth to earth againe.*[12]

The romantic pastiche is followed by what was probably an assigned exercise: an elegy in heroic couplets for Dudley, Lord Carleton, Secretary of State, who died on February 15, 1632. In the years that separated "Constantia and Philetus" from "Pyramus *and* Thisbe," Cowley had done much reading. The underworld scene in the elegy echoes Vergil, Ovid, and Seneca; and the pageant of evil spirits has its counterpart in Spenser's *The Faerie Queene*. The infernal council of "Tartarean *Monsters*"—Revenge, Envy, Boldness, and Rage—who, to *"vex the innocent,"* took Carleton to Death owes a significant debt to sections from Spenser's epic.[13] Indeed, *The Faerie Queene* first taught Cowley to love poetry;[14] but the pagan spirit of his poem (it offers no Christian consolation and is pervaded throughout by a sense of human helplessness) is decidedly non-Spenserian.

The elegy for "Master *Richard Clerke*, late of *Lincolns Inne*," is no less conventional in its adherence to traditional patterns. A single introductory couplet announces the inevitability of death:

"It was decreed by stedfast Destinie, / (The world from Chaos *turn'd) that all should die."* To illustrate the initial statement and to emphasize that all men no matter how famous are subject to the power of fate, a short catalogue celebrates the morality of other great men: *"Roman* Tullie" (Cicero), Solon, and Maro (11. 3-16). In the conventional *laudatio* Cowley lavishes hyperbolic praise on his friend, whose gifts promised to exceed those of Cicero or Solon and whose abilities so far surpassed Vergil's that the great poet would, if he could hear Clerke, *"condemne his* [work] *to fire againe."* The Classical elegy usually concludes with the description of the Elysian fields, but Cowley has combined the arrival into Hades with the Christian arrival into Heaven; his phrase, "Elysiums *lasting Joyes,"* may be pagan, but Angels are there to sing the Requiems: *"But him to* Elysiums *lasting Joyes they bring, / Where winged Angels his sad* Requiems *sing."* Concentrating on death and loss, the elegy narrows to a single line whose terms are sufficiently Christianized to assure promise of another life.

The final poem, "A Dreame of Elysium," is a descriptive catalogue of the landscape of that mythical place. Elysium was, wrote E. K. (his identity remains unknown) in his gloss to the "November Eclogue" of *The Shepherd's Calendar,* "deuised of Poetes to be a place of pleasure like Paradise, where the happye soules doe rest in peace and eternal happynesse."[15] Here grew all things sinless and immaculate, and here were the renowned heroes and lovers of antiquity: Alexander, Horatius, Hero and Leander, Pyramus and Thisbe, Brutus and Portia. Cowley's most delightful passages are those concerned with the floral landscape of this land of eternal spring:

> Here *Hyacinth,* his fate writ in his lookes,
> And thou *Narcissus* loving still the Brookes,
> Once lovely boyes; and *Acis* now a Flower,
> Are nourisht, with that rarer herbe, whose power
> Created thee, Warres potent God, here growes
> The spotlesse Lillie, and the blushing Rose.
> And all those divers ornaments abound,
> That variously may paint the gawdy ground.[16]

The joys of such visions, however, are possessed for only a moment, for *"Thus chiefest Joyes glide with the swiftest streame, / And all our greatest pleasure's but a Dreame."*

"Fit surculus Arbor"—"from the bud comes the tree"—was Cowley's motto for this volume. One cannot expect polished work from one so young, and it is difficult to judge the youthful productions—if, indeed, it is fair to do so—because they are so early. Derivative as the poems are, however, they point to a maker who has read from a long list of Latin and English authors; he had learned his lessons in the traditional genres. Cowley's preference seems to have been for the more paradoxical and fantastical conceits of Ovid and Petrarch rather than for the "plain style" of Ben Jonson. The mannerisms of what Dryden and Johnson were to call the "Metaphysical" could easily develop from the style of "Pyramus *and* Thisbe," and perhaps those characteristics would have won Cowley acclaim from his master, Lambert Osbaldenston.[17] Cowley discovered very early that he had a gift at verses and that he could easily win some reputation through exercising his talent. *Poetical Blossoms* is a schoolboy's collection designed to reveal the precocity of its author.

II "I Went to the University"

In 1636, three years after the first edition of *Poetical Blossoms* and the year he left Westminster, Cowley published an enlarged edition of his first volume, entitled *Sylva, or Divers Copies of Verses, Made upon sundry occasions.* A third edition was published a year later in 1637 when he entered Trinity College. For his title, literally, "The Forest," Cowley had Classical precedent in Statius's *Sylvae* and a nearly contemporary example in the works of Ben Jonson, whose miscellany, "The Forrest," was first published, along with "Epigrammes," in 1616. There are fifteen selections in Jonson's "sylva" (including his fine "To Penhurst," the epistle "To Sir Robert Wroth," and the song, "Come my Celia, let us prove"); songs, epistles, devotional poems, odes, and epodes are all represented. Cowley has sixteen titles in his volume: two occasional poems (one a song) on Charles I and his reign, a translation, six odes, two eulogies, the epistle "A Vote," "A Poetical Revenge," and two elegies.

The occasional poems are not very distinguished productions. The panegyric upon Charles's return from the Scottish coronation in 1633 (and the song on the same) were undoubtedly assigned exercises which Cowley for some reason had retained and included in the volume. In these hyperbolic praises, Charles

is Apollo bringing light back to a darkened land; in gratitude
the citizens' salt tears weep a flood from which arises "*a joyfull
Venus.*" Cowley's poem "*To the Duchesse of Buckingham*" is
of some biographical significance, for it indicates an early rela-
tionship with that influential family. The widowed Duchess, who
is praised for her beauty and nobility, was the mother of George
Villiers, the Second Duke of Buckingham, who was later to
become Cowley's friend and patron.

The other occasional poems, "*To his very much honoured
Godfather, Master* A. B.," "An Elegie on the Death of M^{ris}
[Mrs.] *Anne Whitfield*," and "An Elegie on the Death of *John
Littleton*" are quite conventional. Whenever an occasion pre-
sented itself, even to translate Latin verses on the Blessed Virgin,
Cowley took advantage of it. The interesting and significant
poems, however, are the more personal ones and the half dozen
odes which reveal the strong influence of Horace in form and
theme.

"*A Vote*" (a vow), a poem of eleven stanzas (*a a$_5$ b$_3$ c c$_4$ b$_3$
d d$_5$*), is characterized by an honesty and a simplicity not seen
before in Cowley's verses. The clarity and colloquial nature of
the lines are new, and the conversational tone is well handled.
An attempt to "let all ages heare, . . . / What I abhorre, what I
desire to bee," the poem is Cowley's opportunity to catalogue
professions and to comment satirically upon them; he lists, with
appropriate remarks—one profession to a stanza—those he would
shun. Puritans, pastors by visions, who hope to gain salvation by
"calling th'Pope the Whore of Babylon" are ridiculed, as are
intellectually sterile schoolmasters.

Cowley's final couplet on Justices of the Peace is an excellent
example of his developing satiric technique in employing a fem-
inine rhyme to capture the proper irony; the lines suggest a
couplet from a Gilbert and Sullivan operetta: "And whilst he
mulcts enormities demurely, / Breaks *Priscians* head with sen-
tences securely."[18] Throughout the poem, the reader is aware
that Cowley has learned to handle the concluding couplet more
effectively than he had in "Constantia and Philetus." One's guess
is that he learned something of the power of final couplets from
Ben Jonson's epigrams.

When courtiers who wish "to put off death too, with a Com-
plement" and lawyers "for though they be not blind, they're oft

asleepe," are effectively satirized, the concluding stanzas reveal Cowley's first published Horatian sentiments; and he repeated the lines again many years later in his concluding prose essay, *"Of My self"*:

> This onely grant me: that my meanes may lye
> Too low for envie, for contempt too high.
>   Some honour I would have,
> Not from great deeds, but good alone,
> Th'ignote are better than ill knowne
>   R[u]mor can ope the grave.
> Acquaintance I would hug, but when't depends
> Not from the number, but the choyse of friends.
>
> Bookes should, not businesse, entertaine the light,
> And sleepe, as undisturb'd as death the night.
>   My house a cottage more
> Than palace, and should fitting be
> For all my use, no luxurie.
>   My garden painted ore
> With natures hand, not arts and pleasures yield,
> *Horace* might envie in his *Sabine* field.
>
> Thus would I double my lifes fading space
> For he that runs it well, twice runs his race.
>   And in this true delight,
> These unbought sports, and happy state,
> I would not feare, nor wish my fate,
>   But boldly say each night,
> To morrow let my Sunne his beames display,
> Or in clouds hide them; I have liv'd to day.[19]

Cowley's poem is modeled upon Horace's "Ad Maecenae," in which his Classical mentor also discusses the professions—in commerce and in the military—and voices his preference for rural contentment:

> A man will live happy,
> his own master, when at the close of each day
> he can say "I have lived. Tomorrow
> the Father may fill the heavens with clouds
>
> or with clear sunlight; but never will he turn
> the things that are past to nothing again, nor
> change the pattern and take to pieces
> the gift of a single swift-running hour."[20]

Attracted early to the Horatian viewpoint like his more
famous predecessor at Westminster, Ben Jonson, Cowley unfor-
tunately shows none of the Horatian penchant for "the stylistic
excellence, the sensitive choice of word and phrase, the sense
of proportion and formal 'rightness'—those qualities of tech-
nique, in fine, which have made Horace's commonplaces
'golden.' "[21] What attracted Jonson to Horace was not only the
Horatian temper but also what has come to be known as Horace's
Art of Poetry, a collection of critical remarks which Jonson had
translated twice, once in 1605 and once from Heinsius's text
of 1610. One can only speculate about Cowley's future had he
followed the mode of alumni like Ben Jonson and Thomas Cart-
wright instead of the more flamboyant style of John Donne and
his followers.

Evidence of the early influence of Donne (especially that of
satires I and IV on lawyers and students at the Inns of Court)
may be found in Cowley's "A Poeticall Revenge."[22] Here when
a friend failed to arrive for an appointment arranged at West-
minster, Cowley decided to move

> To the next Court for though I could not know
> Much what they meant, yet I might see and heare
> (As most spectators doe at Theater)
> Things very strange.

When he found a convenient seat from which to watch the pro-
ceedings, a young gallant rudely pushed him from his place. The
speaker's description of this affront is concise and devastating:

> A semi-gentleman of th'Innes of Court,
> In a Sattin suite, redeem'd but yesterday;
> One who is ravisht with a Cock-pit Play,
> Who prayes God to deliver him from no evill
> Besides a Taylors bill, and feares no Devill
> Besides a Serjeant, thrust me from my seat.[23]

"Boy, get you gone, this is no Schoole," he sneered. The boy's
retort is the heart of the "revenge." "Oh no," he replied, "For if it
were, all you gown'd-men would goe / Up for false Latin."
When the "semi-gentleman" raised his hand to strike the impu-
dent boy, he skipped away, flinging out his "darts" in poetry: may
lawyers be cursed with poor Latin, be caught reading Shake-
speare (it is a crime to them to be interested in anything fine),

doomed to be poets, prey to the slow deliberations of physicians, and plagued with poor clients. His "revenge" is all the more effective for the colloquial informality of its accomplished couplets.

The rest of the edition consists of six odes which echo (except for one on Charles) the odes, satires, and epistles of Horace.[24] The first, *"On the praise of Poetry,"* is perfectly conventional. Its form, a_5 a_4 b_5 b_4, had been used by Ben Jonson in his translation of Horace's *Epode* II for *Underwood* in 1640.[25] Emphasizing the immortality of poetry and wit, Cowley reflects Horace's sentiments on the transistory nature of mortal things.[26] Orpheus's songs, one is reminded, are the ultimate poetic accomplishment in "tuning" nature and in making beasts forget "their old Tyrannie"; that music was so exquisitely beautiful that the nightingales themselves could not live and hear it:

> *Nightingales*, harmlesse *Syrens* of the ayre,
> And *Muses* of the place, were there.
> Who when their little windpipes they had found
> Unequall to so strange a sound,
> O'recome by art and griefe they did expire,
> And fell upon the conquering Lyre.
> Happy, ô happy they, whose Tombe might be,
> *Mausolus*, envied by thee![27]

Even the "natural" song of the nightingale passes away; the only immortality is in art.

Ode II, also Horatian,[28] varies the form of the first in its eight quatrains (a_5 a b_4 b_5). The life of a rich and discontented man is likened to an "adulterate Floud" near whose banks no flowers or herbs are found. Such a life is a sterile one in which, as it were, "a perpetuall Winter sterves the ground." What Cowley prizes is a clear, natural life stream, not a gaudy existence laden with treasures not its own. Naturalness and simplicity are central concepts, and one looks to the disciplined and unadorned stream to find a pattern for his own life. The standard is the unity and perfection found in nature; and the clarity of the verse itself, simple and strong, beautifully reflects this Horatian and Jonsonian sentiment:

> Give me a River which doth scorne to shew
> An added beauty, whose cleere brow

May be my looking-glasse, to see
What my face is, and what my mind should be.

Here waves call waves, and glide along in ranke,
    And prattle to the smiling banke.
    Here sad *King fishers* tell their tales,
And fish enrich the Brooke with silver scales.

Dasyes the first borne of the teeming Spring,
    On each side their embrodery bring,
    Here *Lillies* wash, and grow more white,
And *Daffadills* to see themselves delight.

Here a fresh Arbor gives her amorous shade,
    Which *Nature,* the best *Gard'ner* made
    Here I would set, and sing rude layes,
Such as the *Nimphs* and *me my selfe* should please.

Thus I would waste, thus end my carelesse dayes,
    And *Robin-red-brests* whom men praise
    For pious birds, should when I dye,
Make both my *Monument* and *Elegie.*[29]

That what is natural is best is the subject of the four stanzas of Ode III, *"To his Mistris"* ($a\ a_4\ b\ b\ c_3\ c_5$). The poet begins the love song by having the lover ask his lady why she uses cosmetics and jewelry, *"Tryian* dye" and "a golden chayne," when her yellow hair and her sparkling eyes are all the adornment she needs:

I would have all my *Mistris* parts,
    Owe more to *Nature* then to *Arts,*
      I would not woe the dresse,
      Or one whose nights give lesse
      Contentment, then the day.
Shee's faire, whose beauty onely makes her gay.[30]

Cowley's concluding stanza becomes hyperbolic compliment; the metaphor carries the reader into the realm of what it is that makes a "Court / Or pompe." The compression of his figure is worthy of Jonson::'

For 'tis not buildings make a Court
    Or pompe, but 'tis the Kings resort:
      If *Jupiter* downe powre

Himselfe, and in a showre
Hide such bright *Majestie*
Lesse than a *golden one* it cannot be.

In the remaining odes Cowley continues his metrical experiments in form: "On the uncertainty of Fortune" has three stanzas, a_4 b a b_5 c_4 c_5, with the final stanza in the form a_4 b a b_5 c_4 c d d_5; the six stanzas of the ode in commendation of Charles are patterned a a_5 b b_4 c c_3.[31] The poems still seem academic exercises in various stanzaic forms. *"An Answer to an Invitation to Cambridge"* does not repeat a form used before; its three stanzas (a_4 a_5 b_4 b_5 c b c_4 b_3 d d_5) are addressed to John Nicholas, who had been Cowley's senior at Westminster. Nicholas has evidently invited his younger friend to Cambridge, and Cowley was greatly tempted by the "dainties of *Philosophy*" from *"Crambe"* (repetition) at Westminster. The city also calls him with its *"Flagges* and *Pageants"*; and, except for truancy, there seems to be no reason why he stays away:

Why doe I stay then? I would meet
Thee there, but *plummets* hang upon my feet:
'Tis my chiefs wish to live with thee,
But not till I deserve thy company:
Till then wee'l scorne to let that toy,
Some forty miles, divide our hearts:
Write to me, and I shall enjoy,
Friendship, and *wit,* thy better parts.
Though envious *Fortune* larger hindrance brings,
Wee'l easely see each other, *Love hath wings*.[32]

Cowley had shown that he was capable of some sincere personal work, and it is probably no mistake that this poem concludes the volume. The answer to Nicholas makes a dramatic contrast to the conventionality of the poem on Charles with which the volume began. Cowley's precollege volume—it was in its third edition when he went to Trinity—reveals a delight in verse forms and a strong Horatian influence in its obvious fascination with the simple delights of the country: a small house, a small garden, and bucolic peace and quiet.

III   *"Work stolne from Cat or Ball"*

While Cowley was still at Westminster (perhaps in 1634 or 1635), he began a pastoral comedy published in 1638 as *Loves*

Riddle.[33] A fairly tedious and conventional drama in verse and
song of Sicily, its complicated main plot revolves around three
brother-sister groups—Florellus and Callidora, Philistus and Clar-
iana, Aphron and Bellula—all thwarted in love; and at least one
of the group (Bellula) is unaware of her real identity. The com-
plications are resolved and clarified in a crude denouement in
which the lovers are paired off and one discovers that "Turkish
Pyrats" had kidnapped Bellula when she was a child and that the
"ancient Countreyman," Aegon, who had cared for her, was
not her father. The central action of the pastoral, however, con-
cerns Callidora, who, like her more famous predecessor, Beatrice,
disguises herself as a shepherd swain. This masquerade, sug-
gested by the disenchanted clown, Alupis, is the cause of most
of the misunderstandings. Hylace, a country relative of Shake-
speare's Phoebe, and Bellula both woo "Callidorus"—to the dis-
appointment of their lovers, Florellus and Palaemon. The scoun-
drel of the play, Aphron, is more comic than tragic; his
unwelcome attention to Callidora sets the drama in motion and
forces her to flee to the forest. Once he is there, however, his
mad ranting and his myopic praise for the crabbed, lascivious
shepherdess, Truga, are slapstick fun.

There is little to praise in this early dramatic effort except the
figure of Alupis. The love imagery of the play, which has the
lovers freeze one moment and burn the next, and its pastoral
figures indicate conventional literary sources. But Alupis's
trademark is his songs, especially the one he repeats time and
again:

> *Rise up thou mournfull Swaine,*
> *For 'tis but a folly*
> *To be melancholy*
> *And get thee thy pipe againe.*

> *Come sing away the day,*
> *For 'tis but a folly*
> *To be melancholy,*
> *Let's live here whilst wee may.*[34]

One would expect that besides love the concern of pastoral
drama would be the debate over the values of urban and
country life, and carrying on that debate is also part of Alupis's
function. He has been to the city; and, unlike Touchstone,

who prefers the conveniences of the court to the rugged out-
doors of the country, Alupis regards the city as the greater place
of folly. His inheritance had been squandered "to see / What
other Swaines so wondred at, the citie," and now he plays the
"Satyrick Shepheard." While he is the play's commentator on
the foolish and unreasonable behavior of those ruled by love,
it is "Callidorus" who, in soliloquy near the beginning of Act
II, conveys the Horatian theme of the personal advantages of a
life spent in a rural environment:

> How happy is that man, who in these woods
> With secure silence weares away his time!
> Who is acquainted better with himselfe
> Then others; who so great a stranger is
> To Citie follyes, that he knowes them not.
> He sits all day upon some mossie hill
> His rurall throne, arm'd with his crooke, his scepter,
> A flowry garland is his country crowne;
> The gentle lambes and sheepe his loyall subjects,
> Which every yeare pay him their fleecy tribute;
> Thus in an humble statelinesse and majestie
> He tunes his pipe, the woods best melody,
> And is at once, what many Monarches are not,
> Both King and Poet.[35]

Loves Riddle was enthusiastically overrated by Edmund Gosse;
it was, he claimed, "one of the most readable things that Cowley
ever executed. . . . It is written in good blank verse, with con-
siderable sprightliness of dialogue, and with several threads
of intrigues that are held well in hand, and drawn skilfully
together at last."[36] The scene at the close of the second act in
which Aphron praises the hag Truga, who believes his compli-
ments are not without basis in fact, is, Gosse thinks, "a passage
of genuine and delightful humour." Even if one concedes the
humor of that scene, there is some question about the play's
"readability," and there may well have been some question in
Cowley's mind about its quality since he could have included it
in his second or third editions of *Poetical Blossoms* in 1636
or 1637 but decided for some reason to omit it. Its most recent
performance, as Arthur Nethercot notes wryly, was in a version
"adapted by Daniel Bellamy for performance in a young ladies'
boarding school in 1732. Hapless author!"[37]

Gosse's statement about the play's sources is less convincing than his estimate of the play's quality. Cowley followed, he thought, "without imitation," a play by a former Westminster and Trinity College graduate, Thomas Randolph, entitled *The Jealous Lovers*.[38] W. W. Greg has pointed out that there are several ways in which the two plays actually resemble each other; but, while the witch Dipsa may have suggested the figure of Truga, the madness of Aphron finds its parallel in that of Randolph's Amyntas (from a play of the same name). Since many other borrowings might be pointed out, Greg concludes that "convention and petty theft are the warp and woof of the piece."[39] A. H. Nethercot suggests that a closer parallel in plot may be found in Giovanni Guarini's *Il Pastor Fido* (1585),[40] and most readers notice echoes and themes from Terence, Plautus, Sidney, Daniel, and Shakespeare.

One is, therefore, amazed less with the drama itself than with the tremendous scope of reading its sources suggest. Cowley well deserved the epitet "prodigal" at Westminster if by the age of sixteen he had already read the major Classical and contemporary pastoral writers and could compose a play "based entirely on convention and imitation, the sole merit of which was the more or less clever manner in which borrowing, reminiscence, and tradition were interwoven and combined."[41]

If the world of London is never far away from the Sicilian landscape of *Loves Riddle* (there are references to "pritty mistris maukin," the "City Beare-garden," "Welchman," and there is a mad Sicilian who exclaims "Pox on you"[42]), the university world of Cambridge is not far from the next play of Cowley's youth. A five-act Latin comedy set in Dunkirk, *Naufragium Joculare* (*The Comic Shipwreck*), was acted at Trinity on February 2, 1638, and published only a few months later. Cowley himself may have acted in it, as Genest suggests,[43] for the speaker of the prologue comments that the author will appear in a mask—perhaps assuming a role in the play himself.

With little attention to the development of character, the play rests heavily upon Classical figures and plot outlines from Roman comedy. The action is motivated by the shrewd slave, Aemilio, servant to the *miles gloriosus*, Bombardomachides. Aemilio succeeds, along with the help of another shifty servant, in holding the English travelers, Monion, Gelasimus, and their

tutor Gnomicus, "prisoners" while he awaits ransom money
from Monion's father, Polyporus. Aemilio had written to Poly-
porus in his master's name, claiming to have captured the three
in battle. At the conclusion of Act I he had convinced the three
"witwoulds" that they were experiencing a "shipwreck" in a
tavern (an illusion fostered by wine and another wily servant,
Dinon), and he had then made them his prisoners.

In the course of the drama, the familiar *miles* Bombardo-
machides appears with daughter, Eucomissa, her servant, Aegle,
and a sharp-tongued maid, Psecas. To complete the characters
are *filius* Calliphanes and *pater* Calliphanes; the young man is
in love with Aegle but pledged to Eucomissa. After much
hilarity (including a wonderful interlude song by Aemilio and
Dinon), and the discovery that Aemilio and Aegle are the chil-
dren of Polyporus (again "Turkish Pyrats" play a major role),
the couples are paired off: young Calliphanes with Aegle,
Aemilio with Eucomissa, and Psecas with Gelasimus, the
would-be wit.

One of the topical highlights of the play was obviously the
pedant Gnomicus, who, with his two charges, mouths Latin
and Greek phrases and sets up for a wit. In fact, the three are
the founders of a "jesting school," where for a few shillings one
could purchase a string of puns, witty allusions and phrases from
Vergil or Horace to impress others. Pedantic and foolish school-
masters with empty-headed (but rich) pupils never fare well in
farces written and supervised by students. The play ends with
Gnomicus's resolution to return to Cambridge to open his
school there.

The sources of this play are obviously Plautine—there are
echoes of *Stichus, Mostellaria,* and *Captivi*—and one sees ele-
ments from Terence's *Menaechmi.*[44] The machinations of servants,
the satire on pedantry, and the lost child motif all point to
Classical sources. Charles Lamb commented upon a possible
English analogue, a section from Thomas Heywood's *The Eng-
lish Traveller* (1633), which may have given rise to the title of
Cowley's play and supplied it with its central incident in Act
I. Heywood's source, however, was Plautus's *Mostellaria.* John-
son thought the play was written "without due attention to the
ancient models; for it is not loose verse, but mere prose. It was
printed with a dedication in verse to Dr. Comber, master of the

college, but having neither the facility of a popular nor the accuracy of a learned work, it seems to be now universally neglected."[45] Johnson had overlooked Charles Johnson's good English translation (1705) entitled *Fortune in Her Wits*. And he would not have known that Samuel Pepys read the play, perhaps with some delight, a few months before the Restoration, on February 19, 1660: "I took coach home and spent the evening in reading of a Latin play, the 'Naufragium Joculare.'"[46] Modern criticism, if it discusses the play at all, will remember it as the academic piece which precedes Cowley's last schoolboy production, *The Guardian*.

Although *The Guardian* was not published until 1650 (perhaps the fact that it was published then attests to its continued popularity), it was played before Prince Charles at Cambridge on March 12, 1641. Cowley, as the man who could turn out a creditable script in the shortest period, must have been the most promising playwright at Trinity. In the Preface to the edition of poems in 1656, he recalls the hurried circumstances surrounding the preparation of the play; there was

. . .a *Comedy* called *The Guardian*, printed in the year 1650, but made and acted before the *Prince*, in his passage through *Cambridge* towards *York*, at the beginning of the late unhappy War; or rather neither *made* nor *acted*, but *rough-drawn* onely, and *repeated*; for the haste was so great, that it could neither be *revised* or *perfected* by the *Author*, nor *learned without-Book* by the *Actors*, nor set forth in any measure tolerably by the *Officers* of the *College*.

Cowley continues to comment upon a revision which he had begun and then abandoned: "After the *Representation* (which I confess, was somewhat of the *latest*) I began to look it over, and changed it very much, striking out some whole parts, as that of the *Poet* and the *Souldier*; but I have lost the *Copy*, and dare not think it deserves the pains to writ it again. . . . As it is, it is only the hasty *first-setting* of a *Picture*, and therefore like to resemble me accordingly."[47] The play was later revised as the successful Restoration comedy, *Cutter of Coleman Street*.

The Guardian is a loosely constructed comedy of "humours," and most of the characters, out to fleece and cozen their associates, are London ne'er-do-wells. The humor is obvious, sometimes gross; the situations are seldom above the level of slapstick; a great deal of burlesque and boisterous fun are included.

The main plot concerns the thwarted courtship of two unbeliev-
ably stereotyped characters, Young Truman and Lucia, Captain
Blade's ward. Their fidelity, chastity, and complete naïveté
within their corrupt environment are practically unbelievable.

Woven around and through this plot are a series of inter-
related comic episodes: the conquering of the Puritan Tabytha
by the *miles*, Col Cutter; the wedding of pseudo-intellectual Puny
to Aurelia, which is brought about by the machinations of this
neglected and avaricious daughter of Captain Blade; and Blade's
own successful wooing of the rich Puritan widow. The stock
characters and contrived situations—episodes are often too long
and inserted only to provide a bit of topical humor—indicate that
the apologies offered in the prologue are there for reasons other
than modesty or ceremony. Cowley speaks of the play made
"ex tempore" and hopes that the audience will *"Accept our hastie
zeal; a thing that's play'd / Ere 'tis a Play, and acted ere 'tis
made."*[48] He admits that there were "many things in it which I
disliked" and that he made some needed changes in the revised
version."

The inclusion of the Puritan family (Blade's estates have
been mortgaged to the widow) provides part of the play's topical
interest. Blade's daughter, Aurelia, first harangues this family
to her father; when she learns that he hopes to wed the widow,
she satirizes the Puritan household:

Why we shall have all the silenc'd Ministers humming and hawing
thrice a week here; not a dish o' meat but will be longer a blessing
then a rosting. I shall never hear my Virginals when I play upon 'um,
for her daughter *Tabytha's* singing of Psalms. The first pious deed
will be, to banish *Shakespear* and *Ben. Johnson* out of the parlour,
and to bring in their rooms *Mar-prelate*, and *Pryns* works. You'll
ne'er endure 't, Sir. You were wont to have a Sermon once a quarter
at a good time; you shall have ten a day now.[49]

But Cutler's attempt to convince Tabytha that they should be
married is the highlight of the play. Referring to her sanctimoni-
ously as "sister," Cutter appeals to her background. Their mar-
riage, he tells her, was "commanded from above" by "divine
warrant"; in a vision, God Himself commanded the union and
He left behind a marriage license and a "Godly catechism."
"There is," Cutter continues, "a godly Teacher within, that never
was defiled with the Cap and Surplice, never wore that gambol

call'd the Hood; even he shall joyn our hands. Shall we enter, sister?" And Tabytha surrenders: "Brother," she replies, "I'll not resist."[50] As she begins to dance and drink at the festivities following the ceremony, the reader witnesses her complete downfall:

> *Tab.* Here, Duck, here's to all that love us.
> *Col.* A health, you eternal scrapers, sound a health.
>   Bravely done, *Tabytha*: what thinkst thou now
>   o' thy mother?
> *Tab.* A fig for my mother; I'll be a mother my self.
>   Come, Duckling, shall we go home?[51]

In the play, Cowley spares no one: soldiers, lawyers, poets, would-be wits; all the members of the beau monde are included in the comedy. Again it is Aurelia who delivers the stinging commentary on London's pretensions:

But he's [Puny] rich, *Dogrel*, and will be wise enough; when I have got 'um knighted, then I shall be a Lady, *Dogrel;* have a dozen of French-Taylors, Doctors, Jewellers, Perfumers, Tyre-women, to sit in consultation every morning, how I shall be drest up to play at Gleek [a card game], or dance, or see a Comedy, or go to the Exchange i'the afternoon; send every day my Gentleman, to know how such a Lady slept, and dream'd; or whether her dog be yet in perfect health: Then have the young smelling braveries; all adore me, and cut their arms, if I be pleased to be angry: Then keep my close and open Coaches, my yellow sattin Pages, Monkies, and women, or (as they call 'um) creatures.[52]

These individual satiric examples are memorable, but one cannot say that Ben Jonson's models inspired Cowley to any greater productions than had the examples of pastoral and Classical comedy in the two earlier plays.

It is not difficult to see why Cowley's contemporaries were astounded with both the quality and quantity of his early productions. He was able to synthesize his wide reading into mechanical but credible performances; often to do so at very short notice. His was an easy and facile talent, for he seemed to have had no trouble handling the conventions of Ovidian narrative, the more formal public eulogy, or the colloquial Latin drama. His talent was for assimilating the traditions and conventions of his age and of ages past to include in his poems what was most popular at the moment. He pleased his school-masters with his witty, clever, and derivative poems; he was to continue to delight audiences with his extraordinary flair for capturing the latest vogue. Readers most appreciate today the personal poems rather than the great oratorical productions—the scholarly "collages"—which won him immediate fame. When his Muse spoke from Horace she inspired the more enduring poems from this early group.

CHAPTER 2

"The Muses' Hannibal"

I "What shall I do to be forever known"

MANY of the poems Cowley had written since 1638 appear in the *Miscellanies*, the first section of his collected poems of 1656. Except for the verse satire, *The Puritan and the Papist* (1643), and the lyrics of *The Mistress* (1647), the poems are a random sampling from Cowley's work of a fifteen-year period. There are thirty-five selections in the group (including some Cavalier verses and the "Anacreontics"), "some of them made when I was very young, which it is perhaps *superfluous* to tell the *Reader;* I know not by what chance I have kept *Copies* of them; for they are but a very few in comparison of those which I have lost, and I think they have no extraordinary virtue in them, to deserve more care in preservation, then was bestowed upon their *Brethren.*"[1]

The elegies and public poems can be dated, but the other poems span the period from 1638 or 1639 to 1652. All one knows of "The Motto," for instance, is that it was written sometime before 1647 (it was the final poem of *The Mistress*). The second poem, "Ode. *Of Wit*," may belong to 1649 or 1650, when Cowley discussed with Thomas Hobbes and William Davenant the question of wit; more likely the poem originated earlier at Cambridge, in 1638 or 1639, when scholastic debates over wit and composition by negative argument were part of Cowley's academic environment.[2]

The "Ode. *Of Wit*" may have its comic counterpart in Gnomicus and the "witwoulds" of *Naufragium Joculare* (1638). The third poem, *"To the Lord Falkland"* (Lucius Cary), is from 1639, the year of Falkland's return from the Scottish expedition. As one reads, he recognizes very soon that "the *Miscellanies . . .* are arranged chronologically, perhaps having been taken directly from some bound copy-book. . . . The conclusion is strongly presumptive that the intervening, undatable poems also occupy the places where they belong according to time of composition."[3]

To the early period belongs Cowley's poetical discussion of the much debated concept of wit. Jonson, Robert Boyle, Hobbes, Thomas Shadwell and John Dryden made some contribution to the term's history.[4] Young men, says Davenant, associate wit with rhetorical ingenuity; they "imagine it consists in the Musick of words, and beleeve they are made wise by refining their Speech above the vulgar Dialect." Their error is to think of wit in terms of "*Conceits,* things that sound like the knacks or toyes of ordinary *Epigrammatists.*" For old men, on the other hand, wit "lyes in *agnominations,* and in a kinde of an alike tinkling of words, or else in a grave telling of wonderfull things, or in comparing of times without a discover'd partiality."[5]

But, asserts Davenant, "*Wit* is not only the luck and labour, but also the dexterity of thought, rounding the world, like the Sun, with unimaginable motion, and bringing swiftly home to the memory universall surveys."[6] His emphasis, as is Cowley's, is upon the creative and synthetic function of wit: its ability to compose all things into an harmonious and decorous whole. Wit was, as Austin Warren writes, "an instrument of vision. With its occult couplings, it penetrates to the center of the universe, where, however dissimilar they may appear to be unobservant, all things unite."[7] Cowley's poem, with its echoes of Longinus,[8] compares the power of wit to the creative process of divinity.

Although the form of Cowley's ode may come from Donne,[9] his method of definition by negation and elimination is in an old academic tradition. The opening stanza indicates the elusiveness of the subject:

> Tell me, O tell, what kind of thing is *Wit,*
>   Thou who *Master* art of it.
> For the *First matter* loves *Variety* less;
> Less *Women* lov't, either in *Love* or *Dress.*
>   A thousand different shapes it bears,
>   *Comely* in thousand shapes appears.
> Yonder we saw it plain; and here 'tis now
> Like *Spirits* in *a Place,* we know not *How.*[10]

Lines three and four are a hyperbolic comparison in the usual scholastic vein; readers know from Donne and Cowley how women love variety,[11] so now they know that *"First matter"*—

intuition, fancy, wit—loves variety only less than women do;
hence, its love is second only to the principle of variety itself!
The couplet is not to be taken as "wit"; its rhetorical cleverness
is one example of false wit out of whose variety Cowley "builds
a unity."[12] Stanza two, which laments the "*false Ware*" in which
London abounds, claims that men either exaggerate the petty
accomplishments of others or mistake false wit for true. Stanzas
three through seven attack "Metaphysical" poetry. Laughter,
florid talk, forced pentameters (control by "*Inferior Powers*"),
adornment and gilt, jests, anagrams, acrostics, strong lines, "odd
Similitude[s]"—these never indicate true wit. They are the
characteristics of still-born poetry:

> 'Tis not such *Lines* as almost crack the *Stage*
>   When *Bajazet* begins to rage.
> Nor a tall *Meta'phor* in the *Bombast way*,
> Nor the dry chips of short lung'd *Seneca*.
>   Nor upon all things to obtrude,
>   And force some odd *Similitude*.
> What is it then, which like the *Power Divine*
> We only can by *Negatives* define?

"True wit" is discussed in the two concluding stanzas:

> In a true piece of *Wit* all things must be,
>   Yet all things there *agree*.
> As in the *Ark*, joyn'd without force or strife,
> All *Creatures* dwelt; all *Creatures* that had *Life*.
>   Or as the *Primitive Forms* of all
>   (If we compare great things with small)
> Which without *Discord* or *Confusion* lie,
> In that strange *Mirror* of the *Deitie*.
>
> But *Love* that moulds *One Man* up out of *Two*,
>   Makes me forget and injure you.
> I took *you* for *my self* sure when I thought
> That you in any thing were to be *Taught*.
>   Correct my error with thy Pen;
>   And if any ask me then,
> What thing right *Wit*, and height of *Genius* is,
> 'I'll onely shew your *Lines*, and say, '*Tis this*.'[13]

"All things must be" in any work of wit, and all things must
"there *agree*." Cowley argues for an organic product where form

and content so combine that they produce a work which is alive. Since the poem is an analogue of God's creation, it must, like that creation, include all things; like God, the poet becomes an orderer who infuses spirit into his work. *"Of Wit"* is itself proof of the poet's contention, for Cowley successfully blends false wit into a unity which begins to develop from the scholastic conceit of the first stanza.[14] The ode, Johnson thought, was "almost without a rival."[15]

The tribute to Lucius Cary and the elegies for Henry Wotton and Mr. Jordan, second master at Westminster, are the usual occasional poems. More important is the elegy for the Flemish painter, Anthony Van Dyck (1599-1641), whom Cowley may have met at Sir Kenelm Digby's where the artist had been commissioned to do several portraits of Lady Venetia Digby.[16] Cowley valued the painter's great skill, whose "All-resembling *Pencil* did out-pass / The mimick *Imag'ry* of *Looking-glass.*" His was the ability to create the illusion of life, convincing the viewer that, in spite of what he knew, the painting was alive. It was only appropriate that one whose creative abilities were so amazing should witness in heaven the ultimate reality he mirrored so well:

> Thus still he liv'd till heav'n did for him call,
> Where reverent *Luke* salutes him first of all:
> Where he beholds new sights, divinely faire;
> And could almost wish for his *Pencil* there;
> Did he not gladly see how all things shine,
> Wondrously *painted* in the *Mind Divine,*
> Whilst he for ever ravisht with the show
> Scorns his own *Art* which, we admire below.

The contrast between life and painting is continued in the final section:

> Onely his beautcous *Lady* still he loves;
> (The love of heav'nly *Objects Heav'n* improves)
> He sees bright *Angels* in pure beams appear,
> And thinks on her he left so like them here.
> And you, fair *Widow,* who stay here alive,
> Since he so much rejoyces, cease to grieve.
> Your joys and griefs were wont the same to be;
> Begin not now, blest *Pair,* to *Disagree.*

> No wonder *Death* mov'd not his gen'erous mind.
> *You,* and a *new born You,* he left behind.
> Even *Fate* exprest his love to his dear *Wife,*
> And let him end *your Picture* with his *Life.*[17]

Those who live on earth have only the artist to interpret and
mirror reality for them; in death, one joins that first matter which
artists strive to imitate; they leave pictures and poems for their
real counterpart in divinity. The same motif occurs again in the
elegy for Richard Crashaw.

In the group of Cambridge poems is another quite remarkable
elegy, *"On the Death of Mr.* William Hervey." Hervey (1616-42)
had come up to Pembroke Hall in 1638;[18] he took the Bachelor
of Arts in 1639 and the Master's in 1641 and anticipated a prom-
ising future. But his death came suddenly at the college on
May 16, 1642. Cowley and Hervey, young men, had always spent
their time together in serious occupations and pastimes, each
encouraging the other in their academic interests.[19] Perhaps
Cowley went to Hervey with drafts of his poems *"warm* yet
from the *Brain,"* for his friend always "would find out something
to *commend."* The epigraph from Martial, *"Immodicis brevis
est aetas, & rara Senectus"* ("To extraordinary men, life is brief
and old age rare"), is a truth difficult to admit, but Cowley does
it with an honesty and sincerity conveyed simply and directly:

> Ye fields of *Cambridge,* our dear *Cambridge,* say,
> Have ye not seen us walking every day?
> Was there a *Tree* about which did not know
>   The *Love* betwixt us two?
> Henceforth, ye gentle *Trees,* for ever fade;
>   Or your sad branches thicker joyn,
>   And into darksome shades combine,
> *Dark* as the *Grave* wherein my *Friend* is laid.[20]

Charles Lamb found the poem so moving he referred to it as
"Cowley's exquisite Elegy."[21]

The longest poem in *Miscellanies,* the elegy's 152 lines are
divided into nineteen stanzas: $a\ a\ b_5\ b_4\ c_5\ d\ d_4\ c_5$.[22] (The tetra-
meter lines four and seven sometimes become trimeters.) Stan-
zas one through three emphasize the personal loss of a "sweet
Companion, and . . . gentle *Peere."* The third stanza concludes
with the traditional question: "Alas, my *Treasure's* gone, why

do I stay?" Stanzas four through nine describe the depth of friendship and the joys experienced together, and the turning point is reached in the tenth stanza. Its antithetical imagery of "high" and "low" plays upon the physical "lowness" of death and earthly life which have been the twin centers of the opening stanzas and upon the metaphoric "highness" achieved now in death and foreshadowed by his earthly achievements:

> Large was his *Soul;* as large a *Soul* as ere
> Submitted to *inform* a *Body* here.
> High as the Place 'twas shortly'in *Heav'n* to have,
>   But low, and humble as his *Grave.*
> So *high* that all the *Virtues* there did come
>   As to their chiefest seat
>   Conspicuous, and great;
> So *low* that for *Me* too it made a room.

This antithesis, Loiseau comments,

with its symmetrical opposition of terms, gives a medal-like relief to his poetic line. The harmony of balanced movement is combined with energy and clarity. The oratorical and intellectual tendencies of his poetry are thus asserted in the general characteristics of his style. Thought takes precedence over feeling, eloquence replaces lyicism.[23]

Loiseau echoes Johnson's comment that there is "little passion" in the poem, but it is not without its lyric moments; and, as one reads the final stanzas which form the Classic *laudatio* and *consolatio,* he is convinced that Hervey, blessed in heaven in the company of saints, continues his life on a higher level:

> But happy Thou, ta'ne from this frantick age,
>   Where *Igno'rance* and *Hypocrisie* does rage!
> A fitter *time* for Heav'n no soul ere chose,
>   The place now onely free from those.
> There 'mong the *Blest* thou dost for ever shine,
>   And wheresoere thou casts thy view
>   Upon that white and radiant crew,
> See'st not a *Soul* cloath'd with more *Light* then Thine.

> And if the glorious *Saints* cease not to know
> Their wretched friends who *fight* with *Life* below;
> Thy Flame to *Me* does still the same abide,
>   Onely more pure and rarifi'd.

> There whilst immortal Hymns thou dost reherse,
>   Thou dost with holy pity see
>   Our dull and earthly *Poesie*
> Where *Grief* and *Mis'ery* can be join'd with *Verse*.[24]

Composed almost a decade later are Cowley's significant verses
"*To Sir* William Davenant. *Upon his two first Books of* Gondi-
bert, *finished before his voyage to* America."[25] Cowley met the
celebrated wit while they were both in exile and attached to the
Jermyn family in the Louvre. "Jolly Will," the dissolute godson
of Shakespeare, was the frequent butt of his companions' jests.
Suckling's *A Sessions of the Poets* alluded to his nose (deformed
by mercury treatments to cure syphilis) while describing him

>   . . . Asham'd of a foolish mischance
> That he had got lately travelling in *France,*
> Modestly hoped the handsomenesse of's Muse
> Might any deformity about him excuse

>   And
> Surely the Company would have been content
> If they could have found any President;
> But in all their Records, either in Verse or Prose,
> There was not one Laureat without a nose.[26]

Davenant, before leaving France for the Maryland colony of
which Charles had appointed him governor, had completed
the first two books of his epic poem, *Gondibert*.[27] His great
accomplishment, Cowley thought, was in banishing the "fantas-
tick *Fairy Land*" from the realm of the epic:

> Methinks *Heroick Poesie* till now
> Like some fantastick *Fairy Land* did show,
> *Gods, Devils, Nymphs, Witches* and *Gyants race,*
> And all but *Man* in *Mans chief work* had place.
> Thou like some worthy *Knight* with sacred Arms
> Dost drive the *Monsters* thence, and end the *Charms.*

The elimination of supernatural machinery made room for "*Men*
and *Manners* . . . , / The things which that rich *Soil* did chiefly
want." Developing a contrast between the events of his age
which saw the destruction of "present *Empires*" and the past
brought alive by the divine poet, Cowley suggests a paradox
based upon the *felix culpa*:

So will our God *rebuild* man's perisht frame,
And raise him up much *Better*, yet the *same*.
So *God-like Poets* do past things reherse,
Not *change*, but *Heighten* Nature by their verse.

Cowley's emphasis is upon nature as a standard, nature "not changed," but brought into sharper focus and organized through art; what he praised in Van Dyck's paintings is what he praises here: the artist's gift in ordering his materials without changing their naturalness. Cowley recognizes in Davenant a "standard of nature and truth [and] the simple clarity of style that it enjoins . . . [which] mark[s] the end of the older poetry and herald[s] the Augustan."[28] Davenant had discovered a new world for verse:

Sure 'twas this noble boldness of the *Muse*
Did thy desire to seek new *Worlds* infuse,
And ne'er did Heav'n so much a *Voyage* bless,
If thou canst *Plant* but *there* with like success.

Unfortunately, his sea voyage was not a success,[29] but he had made Cowley aware of new standards for the epic; perhaps it was the baroque poetry of Richard Crashaw that suggested the significance of the religious setting for a poem like the *Davideis*.

"*On the Death of Mr.* Crashaw" closes the section of original poems in the *Miscellanies*. Johnson thought the lines to "excel all that have gone before them, and in which there are beauties which common authors may justly think not only above their attainment, but above their ambition."[30] This praise for the elegy is very high, but not undeserved. Cowley had known Richard Crashaw (1612-49) from undergraduate days,[31] and Crashaw's tribute to the younger poet's talents, "*Upon two green Aprocockes sent to* Cowley *by Sir* Crashaw," suggests that the older student may have sought out the boy who came to Cambridge already having published a book of poems:

. . . O had my wishes
And the deare merits of your Muse, their due,
The yeare had found some fruit early as you;
Ripe as those rich composures time computes
Blossoms, but our blest tast confesses fruits.
How does thy April-Autumn mocke these cold
Progressions 'twixt whose termes poor time grows old?

> With thee alone he weares no beard, thy braine
> Gives him the morning worlds fresh gold againe.
> 'Twas only Paradice, 'tis onely thou,
> Whose fruit and blossoms both blesse the same bough.[32]

With the Civil War, Crashaw was forced to the Continent;[33] the decade 1640 saw him at Leyden (?); back to Oxford, Paris, Rome; and finally at Loretto, where he died on August 21, 1649. The news did not reach Cowley until 1651 when he began the elegy:

> *Poet* and *Saint!* to thee alone are given
> The two most sacred *Names* of *Earth* and *Heaven.*
> The hard and rarest *Union* which can be
> Next that of *Godhead* with *Humanitie.*
> Long did the *Muses* banisht *Slaves* abide,
> And built vain *Pyramids* to mortal pride;
> Like *Moses* Thou (though Spells and Charms withstand)
> Hast brought them nobly home back to their *Holy Land.*[34]

With these balanced, stately couplets the poem proceeds in praise of Crashaw in heaven. Because he always sang with angels while he was on earth, his death represents no dramatic change in environment for him; in heaven, he need only sing his old songs. His condition is heightened, not changed; he is different, yet the same. In spite of his example, earth remains the place where "*old Heathen Gods* in *Numbers* dwell," and where poets,

> (Vain men!) the *Monster Woman Deifie;*
> Find *Stars,* and tye our *Fates* there in a *Face,*
> And *Paradise* in them by whom we *lost* it, place.
> What different faults corrupt our *Muses* thus?
> *Wanton* as *Girles,* as *old Wives, Fabulous!*

Crashaw lived untouched by that profane muse who inspired lesser poets than he, for his muse was spotless and, paradoxically, "A fruitful *Mother* was, and *Virgin* too." As the poem becomes progressively more colloquial, its intensity increases in a fine passage on the circumstances of Crashaw's death:

> How well (blest Swan) did Fate contrive thy death;
> And made thee render up thy tuneful breath
> In thy great *Mistress* Arms? thou most divine
> And richest *Off'ering* of *Loretto's Shrine!*
> Where like some holy *Sacrifice* t'expire,

> A *Fever* burns thee, and *Love* lights the *Fire*.
> *Angels* (they say) brought the fam'ed *Chappel* there,
> And bore the sacred Load in Triumph through the air.
> 'Tis surer much they brought thee there, and *They*
> And *Thou*, their charge, went *singing* all the way.

Apologizing for Crashaw's Catholicism, "His *Faith* perhaps in some Tenets might / Be wrong; his *Life*, I'm sure, was *in the right*," Cowley ends conventionally by asking for inspiration from Crashaw's spirit:

> Thou from low earth in nobler *Flames* didst rise,
> And like *Elijah*, mount *Alive* the skies.
> *Elisha*-like (but with a wish much less,
> More fit thy *Greatness* and my *Littleness*)
> Lo here I beg (I whom thou once didst prove
> So humble to *Esteem*, so Good to *Love*)
> Not that thy *Spirit* might on me *Doubled* be,
> I ask but *Half* thy mighty *Spirit* for Me.
> And when my *Muse* soars with so strong a Wing,
> 'Twill learn of things *Divine*, and First of *Thee* to sing.

The final Alexandrine is a perfect conclusion, and Geoffrey Walton's statement aptly summarizes the course of the elegy: "Cowley has brought his feelings to order and harmony in a mood of rapt contemplation. He started formally, and, after working with Neo-Classic *ordonnance* through various moods of simplicity and intimacy, he returns to a rigid convention."[35]

II *"Enjoy the Present Hour"*

The last section of "Miscellanies" is a group of eleven free translations from Anacreon and a final "Elegie upon Anacreon, Who was choaked by a Grape-Stone." Translations from the *Anacreontea* were very popular in the middle seventeenth century; Jonson, Robert Herrick, Edward Sherburne, and others had worked from the popular text edited by Henri Estienne, *Anacreontis Teii odae* (Paris, 1554). Cowley's delightful irregularly accented octosyllabic couplets were, Gosse thought, "frequently pretty and sparkling";[36] but Johnson was even more generous with his praise:

The Anacreon of Cowley, like the Homer of Pope, has admitted the decoration of some modern graces, by which he is undoubtedly more

amiable to common readers, and perhaps, if they were justly to
declare their own perceptions, to far the greater part of those whom
courtesy and ignorance are content to style the Learned.

These little pieces will be found more finished in their kind than
any other of Cowley's works. The diction shews nothing of the mould
of time, and the sentiments are at no great distance from our present
habitudes of thought.[37]

Comparison with other contemporary translations by Richard
Lovelace and Thomas Stanley reveals what it was that so
charmed Johnson.

"*The Grasshopper*" is an excellent example of Cowley's
method: light, simple, clear and direct, it never loses sight
of its object while it contemplates time and happiness. Richard
Lovelace's version in quatrains is a more philosophical, obscure,
and involved poem on the joys of friendship; and Thomas Stan-
ley's is a more literal translation of Anacreon's Latin and about
half the length of Cowley's version. Here is Cowley's translation:

> Happy *Insect*, what can be
> In happiness compar'd to Thee?
> Fed with nourishment divine,
> The dewy *Mornings* gentle *Wine!*
> *Nature* waits upon thee still,
> And thy verdant Cup does fill,
> 'Tis fill'd where ever thou dost tread,
> *Nature* selfe's *thy Ganimed.*
> Thou dost drink, and dance, and sing;
> Happier then the happiest *King!*
> All the *Fields* which thou dost see,
> All the *Plants* belong to *Thee,*
> All that *Summer Hours* produce,
> Fertile made with early juice.
> Man for thee does sow and plow;
> *Farmer He,* and *Land-Lord Thou!*
> Thou dost innocently joy;
> Nor does thy *Luxury* destroy;
> The *Shepherd* gladly heareth thee,
> More *Harmonious* then *He.*
> Thee Country Hindes with gladness hear,
> *Prophet* of the ripened year!
> Thee *Phoebus* loves, and does inspire;
> *Phoebus* is himself thy *Sire.*
> To thee of all things upon earth,

> *Life* is no longer then thy *Mirth.*
> Happy *Insect*, happy *Thou*,
> Dost neither *Age*, nor *Winter* know.
> But when thou'st drunk, and danc'd, and sung,
> Thy fill, the flowery Leaves among
> (*Voluptuous*, and *Wise* with all,
> *Epicurean Animal!*)
> Sated with thy *Summer Feast*,
> Thou retir'st to endless *Rest.*[38]

The ageless, "careless" insect leads a life man can covet but never acquire. Cowley's lyric is a nostalgic evocation of this natural singer who inherits the earth but who has known none of the fears and fatigues of human kind.

The translations are not always so fortunate, for at the opposite extreme is the awkward and less graceful *"Gold."* Stanley's version of this Latin poem by Anacreon is again the more economical and literal of the two. Cowley's expanded treatment, with its repetitive and uncontrolled series of syntactic parallels, is an unsuccessful exercise in rhetorical repetition; the following excerpt characterizes the awkwardness:

> A *curse* on him who found the Ore!
> A *curse* on him who digg'd the store!
> A *curse* on him who did refine it!
> A *curse* on him who first did coyn it!
> A *curse* all curses else above.[39]

Cowley's versions are seldom so boisterous, however. There is the modulated and sentimental

> *Love* smil'd, and from my'enfeebled *Lyre*
> Came gentle airs, such as inspire
> Melting love, soft desire.
> Farewel then *Heroes*, farewel *Kings*,
> And mighty *Numbers*, mighty *Things*:
> Love tunes my *Heart* just to my *strings.*[40]

In the episodic *"Age"* Cowley laments his graying hair and advancing age, noting that

> 'Tis time short pleasures now to take,
> Of little *Life* the best to make,
> And manage *wisely* the *last stake.*[41]

He sings the "familiar and the festive"[42] in *"The Epicure"*:

> Fill the *Bowl* with rosie Wine,
> Around our temples *Roses* twine.
> And let us chearfully awhile,
> Like the *Wine* and *Roses* smile.[43]

Lastly, the comic *"The Account,"* offers a fantastic Leporello-like tally of loves from every country and every clime: Athens, Corinth, Chios, Lesbos, Rhodes, Crete, Syria, and on and on. This version from Anacreon has its relative in *"The Chronicle,"* a catalogue of mistresses with a delightful series of witty surprises and personal allusions that keeps the reader guessing what will come next.[44] Each stanza traces the course of a new romance and a new mistress (Margarita, Martha, Judith, Susanna, Isabella, and others) as Cowley playfully ransacks all the conventional conceits with which to image the lovers' relationship. Judith holds *"Soveraign Power"* over his heart until it, challenged by the "Artillery" of Isabella's eye, found Judith unfit to govern. Anarchy threatened the reign of Isabella, however, when Besse entered the commonwealth created by love.[45] With such traditional metaphors, Cowley sustains one of his most successful attempts at lighthearted verse. Whether the many ladies are identifiable or not—and Nethercot's suggestions that the names may be associated with persons in the poet's life are as tantalizing as the poem[46]—the mock-heroic lyric remains one of Cowley's most satisfying productions. Recounting the behavior associated with lovers, this poem looks forward to what comes in the second section of the great edition—the love poems of *The Mistress*, where one learns of

> . . . the politick Arts
> To take and keep mens hearts
> The Letters, Embassies, and Spies,
> The Frowns, and Smiles, and Flatteries,
> The Quarrels, Tears, and Perjuries,
> Numberless, *Nameless Mysteries!*[47]

CHAPTER 3

"The great *Methusalem* of *Love*"

I "Love's Professor"

T HE second section of Cowley's collected works was a group
of poems published previously in 1647—the year an enter-
prising London printer published the small octavo volume, *The
Mistress*, an allegedly unauthorized edition of Cowley's love lyr-
ics.[1] Two years earlier, in 1645, Edmund Waller had celebrated
his lady; in 1646, John Suckling and James Shirley published love
poems; in 1647, there were collections by John Hall and Thomas
Stanley; and, in 1648, Robert Herrick issued his songs, *The
Hesperides*. Both Cowley and publisher, well aware of the fashion
in love verses, considered the moment opportune.

Cowley was in France when the poems appeared, and he had
probably written most of them in the two years preceding pub-
lication. Forced to leave Cambridge in April, 1643, because of
Civil War politics, he had first taken refuge at Oxford; and, hav-
ing later assumed the post of secretary to Henry, Lord Jermyn,
who was the Queen's Chamberlain, he made his way to Paris.
Since Henrietta Maria left England in the spring of 1644 (and
Oxford fell to Parliamentary forces in June, 1644), it is safe to
assume that, if Jermyn and Cowley did not accompany her,
they soon followed. For a little more than a decade Cowley
remained abroad, one of a large circle of expatriates which in-
cluded William Davenant (at work on *Gondibert*), John Evelyn,
Richard Crashaw (who preceded Cowley to the Continent),
and Edmund Waller. *The Mistress* would establish Cowley's
lady "next in fame / To *Sacharissas* well-sung name."[2] Undoubt-
edly, Cowley's desire to please and entertain his new group of
friends also prompted his venture into this genre. Although it
is possible, it is not likely that the poems were motivated by a
genuine love affair.

In the Preface composed for the 1656 folio, Cowley confesses that he thought of the love poems as an obligation he owed to his vocation as poet; "for so it is," he explains, "that *Poets* are scarce thought *Free-men* of their *Company,* without paying some duties, and obliging themselves to be true to *Love.* Sooner or later they must all pass through that *Tryal,* like some *Mahumetan Monks,* that are bound by their Order, once at least, in their life, to make a *Pilgrimage* to *Meca, In furias ignèmq; ruunt; Amor omnibus idem*"[3] (All rush to this fiery madness; love is alike for all.) To insure that the reader makes no mistake that a persona is involved, Cowley emphasizes the poetic "mask"; "he [the poet] may be in his own practice and disposition a *Philosopher,* nay a *Stoick,* and yet speak sometimes with the softness of an amorous *Sappho.*" He concludes the section in defense of the language and tone of his poems:

Neither would I here be misunderstood, as if I affected so much gravity, as to be ashamed to be thought really in *Love.* On the contrary, I cannot have a good opinion of any man who is not at least capable of being so. But I speak it to excuse some expressions (if such there be) which may happen to offend the severity of supercilious *Readers;* for much *Excess* is to be allowed in *Love,* and even more in *Poetry*; so we avoid the two unpardonable vices in both, which are *Obscenity* and *Profaneness,* of which I am sure, if my *words* be ever guilty, they have ill represented my thoughts and intentions.[4]

Nothing in *The Mistress* could possibly offend a modern audience (or a post-Restoration reader accustomed to Charles Sedley and John Rochester); but such a defense, written while Cowley was in prison, was a cautious, politic move for one who wished to ingratiate himself with the authorities. There was, however, at least one bigoted attack in 1670, when Edmund Elys, who saw himself as "a dutiful son of the church," proclaimed *The Mistress* to be "lascivious and profane."[5] Readers today will undoubtedly congratulate Cowley on his restraint in a period notorious for its more salacious productions.

Cowley's love poems are, as he admits, evidence of his apprenticeship in the tradition. Whether he ever suffered the "great Passion" is perhaps an irrelevant literary question (although not to Johnson, who thought that, because Cowley was only in love once, "and then never had resolution to tell his passion," "this consideration cannot but abate in some measure the reader's esteem for the work and the author"),[6] and there is only slim and slightly circumstantial evidence for the positive assumption. Cowley's comment in his essay *"Of Greatness"* is part of that evidence: "If I were ever to fall in love *again* [italics mine]," he writes, "(which is a great Passion, and therefore, I hope, I have done with it . . .)."[7] This statement is the only primary evidence in the work itself.

Joshua Barnes, who mentions Cowley in his eighteenth-century edition of Anacreon, is responsible for some "embroidery" on the comment that the poet had been in love; Cowley, Barnes claimed, was too shy to declare himself.[8] There is no reason to assume that either of these "loves" (if there were two, or even one) was the one celebrated in *The Mistress;* and the "portrait" of the lady there, hidden as she is behind the conventions, does not aid the biographer's search. Upon these slim contentions most of the argument rests.

But in Samuel W. Singer's edition of Joseph Spence's *Anecdotes, Observations, and Characters, of Books Collected from the Conversations of Mr. Pope, and other Eminent Persons of his Time,*[9] there is one additional bit of evidence. There Pope is reported to have said that the lady in question later became the wife of Thomas Sprat's brother.[10] But, as A. H. Nethercot points out, "It is extremely unlikely that these two ladies were the same, since Sprat was seventeen years younger than Cowley and the two men did not meet until nearly a decade after the main series of the lyrics was published in 1647."[11] The lady in the poems has more affinities with her literary predecessors—Petrarch's Laura and Waller's Sacharissa—than she has with any real "mistress" in the poet's life.

II *"Teach me to Love?"*

The eighty-three lyrics in the complete edition (there were seventy-six in the 1647 collection)[12] dramatically record the vicissitudes of the romance until it is obvious that the lady has finally yielded to the passionate entreaties and equivocating pleas of her clever lover. "DIALOGUE" is the poetical record of her reactions after her surrender; at first protesting that she has been undone and "robb'd" by a lover who has stolen *"Illgotten Treasure,"* she cries out over her loss:

> What have we done? what cruel passion mov'd thee,
>   Thus to ruine her that lov'd Thee?
> *Me* thou'hast *robb'ed,* but what art thou
> Thy *Self* the *richer* now?
>   *Shame* succeeds the short-liv'd *pleasure;*
> So soon is spent, and gone, this thy *Ill-gotten Treasure.*
>
> ·
>
> No: I'm undone; my Honour Thou hast slain,
>   And nothing can restore't again.
> Art and Labour to bestow,
> Upon the *Carcase* of it now,
>   Is but t'embalm a body *dead,*
> The *Figure* may remain, the *Life* and *Beauty's* fled.[13]

The lover argues that she view it not as theft on his part but as charity on hers. Finally the lady appears to be won over by his artful equivocation, and in playful paradox she concludes the witty repartee:

> *Curse* on thine *Arts!* methinks I *Hate* thee now;
>   And yet I'm sure I *love Thee* too!
> I'm *angry,* but my *wrath* will prove,
> More *Innocent* than did thy *Love.*
>   Thou hast *this day* undone me quite;
> Yet wilt undo me more should'st thou not come at *night.*[14]

The careful phrasing of the final Alexandrine emphasizes rhetorically the melodramatic opposition in the dialogue between triumph and disaster, while the witty effect of the second half of the line underscores the comic irony of the preceding debate. The traditional arguments for chastity are devastated in the banter of an urbane, sophisticated lady who protests too much.

Throughout the series the courtier has little but sarcasm for platonic love, and he toys ironically with the platonic admission that the body is essential to the recognition of the beauty of the soul. But, he argues, to dismiss the body when that stage is reached is to do it a great injustice; exclusive love of the soul is for angels only, and "When I'm *all soul,* such shall *my Love* too be."[15] The arguments against platonic love are presented in the eighth lyric, *"Platonick Love."* Cowley's opening couplet, "Indeed I must confess, / When *Souls* mix 'tis an *Hap-*

piness," begins what one might consider a flippant and sar-
castic reply to John Donne's famous neo-platonic argument,
"The Extasie." Conceding that happiness can be achieved through
the love of one soul for another, the speaker plays with Donne's
favorite oppositions of body and soul and unity and variety to
defend carnal love.

The use of Donne's method of devious argumentation in
other poems where the opposite kind of love is proposed sug-
gests that Cowley may have suspected Donne's sincerity but
was fascinated with his technique. Donne's lover does not deny
the validity of physical love; he views it as an intermediary
but necessary step to a greater ecstasy experienced while the
physical powers of the body are suspended. Donne's speaker
claims that love is complete only when souls combine, but
Cowley's version reverses this attitude by implying that, after
all is said, happiness is not complete until the bodies "combine."
Donne's poem has, Cowley implies, underplayed the body's role,
and he wants to be sure physical love is not underrated:

> That *souls* do beauty know,
>   'Tis to the *Bodies* help they owe;
> If when they know't, they strait abuse that trust,
> And shut the *Body* from't, 'tis as unjust,
> As if I brought my dearest *Friend* to see
> My *Mistress,* and at th'instant *He*
>   Should steal her quite from *Me.*[16]

In *The Mistress,* the "model" is consistently to be found in
Donne's *Songs and Sonets* (1633). In some poems—"*The Spring,*"
"*The Wish,*" and "*For Hope*"—the influence is relatively minor.
John Sparrow, who has pointed out instances of actual imitation,
specifies how "Donne's influence determines the form, the open-
ings, the titles of the poems, and might often be said to dictate
their subject."[17] One is immediately aware of Cowley's habit of
direct outburst in the initial line of a poem:

> "By heaven I'll tell her boldly that 'tis She"
>   (*"The Discovery"*)

> "No; thou'rt a fool, I'll swear, if e're thou grant"
>   (*"Against Fruition"*)

"For Heavens sake, what d'you mean to do"
　　　(*"The Same,"* following *"Resolved
　　　to be Beloved"*)

"Teach *me* to *Love?* go teach thy self more wit"
　　　(*"The Prophet"*)

"Ha! ha! you think y'have *kill'd my fame"*
　　　(*"Called Inconstant"*)

In addition, there are quite overt echoes found if one compares
the following poems from *The Mistress* with their counterparts
in Donne's work: *"Inconstancy"* with "Woman's Constancy";
"Platonick Love" with "The Extasie"; *"My Dyet"* with "Loves
Diet"; *"Love and Life"* (stanza one) with "The Computation";
"The Given Heart" (stanza two) with "Loves Infiniteness"
(stanza two); *"The Prophet"* (stanza one) with "The Will";
"My Picture" (stanza one) with "Elegy V"; *"The Encrease"*
(stanza one) with "Loves Growth"; *"The Heart Breaking"* with
"The Broken Heart"; *"Maidenhead"* (stanza four) with "Loves
Alchymie"; *"The Inconstant"* with "The Indifferent."[18]
　　The two final examples are very close imitations if one com-
pares the following stanza from Cowley's *"Maidenhead"* with
its counterpart in Donne's "Loves Alchymie":

> Although I think thou never found wilt be,
> 　　Yet I'm resolv'd to search for thee;
> 　　The search it self rewards the pains.
> So, though the *Chymick* his great *secret* miss,
> (For neither it in *Art* nor *Nature* is)
> 　　Yet things well worth his toyle he gains;
> 　　And does his Charge and Labour pay
> With good *unsought exper'iments* by the way.[19]

Or one has the following representative stanza from Cowley's
"The Inconstant" to compare with Donne's "The Indifferent":

> The *Fat,* like *Plenty,* fills my heart;
> 　　The *Lean,* with *Love* make me too so.
> If *Streight,* her *Body's Cupid's Dart*
> 　　To me; if *Crooked,* 'tis his *Bow.*
> Nay *Age* it self does me to rage encline,
> And strength to *Women* gives, as well as *Wine.*[20]

Significantly, this stanza is preceded by two in which the speaker proclaims he can love any and all, regardless of color, shape, stature, or fairness; he can find in all women something commendable—some goodness, wit, or grace to attract him. Emphasizing similarities between two poets who both love the paradox, the daring hyperbole, and the extended and complex conceit reveals Cowley as a brilliant and successful imitator of Donne's manner.

In the main group of poems, the lack of any apparent ordering of the lyrics indicates that Cowley had no intention of presenting a consistent "cycle"; his major concern was the ingenuity of separate poems, not the group as a whole.[21] From the poems, however, one can piece together the parts of the conventional drama; and, in Loiseau's phase, one discovers that "The poet has no desire to take any initiative [therein]. He remains resolutely within tradition, ready to enhance by one the long line of poets who since Petrarch have sung of the sweet tortures of love."[22]

Cold, haughty, aloof, inconstant, arbitrary, "murderous" in her refusal to recognize the ardor of her lover, the noble lady refuses for some time even to admit his existence. The spirited and indefatigable lover is alternately humble, brusque, cajoling, jeering, contrite, angry, patient, sarcastic, and suffering. The course of his romance is traditional; the discovery that he has a wealthy rival is occasion for an "epistle," "*The rich Rival.*" The quiet conversational tone delivers a final devastating insult:

> They say you're angry, and rant mightilie,
>   Because I love the same as you;
>   Alas! you're very *rich;* 'tis true;
> But prithee Fool, what's that to *Love* and *Me?*
>   You'have *Land* and *Money,* let that serve;
>   And know you'have more by that than you *deserve.*[23]

As he continues his insult, the poet-speaker promises to conquer his rival's family connections and wealth with his own "noble *verse*" and rhetoric, which, he adds sarcastically, his competitor does not (or cannot) understand. In his last stanza, however, the speaker, having become more and more boisterous, reveals that he is the only "genuine" lover among the threesome; for he doubts that the lady loves him at all. Even she, he intimates, has been won over by the friends and "blood" of the rival. Cowley probably intended that the revelation of the lady's love for the rival would reinforce the drama of the lyric, but the speaker is apparently too concerned with the rival to worry over the lady. Cowley emphasizes only the situation, seldom developing any kind of psychological drama.

Continuing in the collection, one reads of a temporary separation ("*The Parting*"), an occasion for a secret love letter ("*Written in Juice of Lemon*"), the lady's accusation of disloyalty with her maid ("*The Waiting Maid*"), and a meditation on a memento ("*The Picture*")—all are familiar subjects for love lyrics. Satisfied to remain within the range of popular tastes and fancies in subject matter, Cowley seems uninterested in inventing unique or original topics. He was content to follow the way of Donne.

Working in Donne's manner, however, can be as exciting as it is dangerous, for the poet's enthusiasms for a method may not always sustain his productions. Especially illustrative of this weakness are two poems about time in a lover's existence, where Cowley attempts sustained intellectual argument. Very much "un professeur d'amour,"[24] rather than the lover himself, he lectures about "*Love and Life*":

> Not that *Loves* Hours or Minutes are
> Shorter than those our *Being's* measur'ed by:
>   But they're more close *compacted* far,
>   And so in lesser room do lye.
> Thin airy things extend themselves in space,
>   Things *solid* take up little place.
>
> Yet *Love,* alas, and *Life* in Me,
> Are not two several things, but purely one,
>   At once how can there in it be
>   A double *different Motion?*
> O yes, there may: for so the self same *Sun,*
>   At once does slow and swiftly run.
>
> Swiftly his *daily* journey 'he goes,
> But treads his *Annual* with a statelier pace,
>   And does three hundred Rounds enclose
>   Within one yearly Circles space.
> And once with *double course* in the same *Sphaere,*
>   He *runs* the *Day,* and *Walks* the *year.*[25]

These representative stanzas indicate something of the manner which is the important feature. The pressure of an immediate occasion is lost as the speaker engages in an extended meditation on love and time; the interest is not in the romance itself but in the realm of argument. The *idea* of love and time interests the lover while the figures reveal no passion or emotion. The situation is, in other words, static. Time for lovers, one learns, is "more close *compacted* far" than the hours and minutes of life. Life creeps by solar time when one thinks of the sun in terms of its yearly journey; however, when one thinks of the sun moving rapidly in its daily course, he has some concept of the speed of time to the lover. The "time" of life moves slowly and is expansive; the "time" of love is rapid and compact, and both his love and his life find their ultimate values in his soul. The conclusion is reached in a witty and suggestive pun on "soul" and "sol." But all this discussion cannot rescue *"Love and Life"*; it is an adequate but dull poem, an excellent example of what can happen to the style of Donne in Cowley's hands. Without vivacity and wit, its argument plods along in a pedestrian manner. The poet's models can prove as overpowering as they are inspiring.

A companion poem, *"The Iong Life,"* is more successful. Extending a less complex metaphor through six stanzas, the lover realizes that his life is, as it were, "out of order":

> The various *Motions* of the turning *Year,*
>   Belong not now at all to Me:
> Each *Summers Night* does *Lucies* now appear,
>   Each *Winters* day *St. Barnaby.*

Having grown "old" in love, his age, in that respect, is artificially lengthened and approaches that of the Patriarchs. His plea is to be "brought back" to the normal order of time:

> Sure those are happy people that complain,
>   O th' *shortness* of the days of man:
> Contract mine, Heaven, and bring them back again.
>   To th' ordinary *Span.*[26]

The love of argumentation and its consequent development are still apparent, but the poem's relative simplicity rescues it from the fate of *"Love and Life."*

Cowley's best efforts are fine samples of his ability to trans-

form Donne's mode into his own idiom: *"The Prophet"* is a
virtuoso example:

> Teach *me* to *Love*? go teach thy self more wit;
>   I chief *Professour* am of it.
>   Teach craft to *Scots*, and thrift to *Jews*,
>   Teach boldness to the Stews;
> In *Tyrants* Courts teach supple *flattery*,
> Teach *Jesuits*, that have *travell'd* far, to Lye.
>   Teach Fire to burn, and Winds to blow,
>   Teach restless Fountains how to flow,
>   Teach the dull earth, fixt, to abide,
> Teach *Woman-kind* inconstancy and Pride.
> See if your diligence here will useful prove;
> But, pr'ithee, teach not me to *Love*.
>
> The *God* of *Love*, if such a thing there be,
>   May learn to love from *Me*.
>   He who does boast that he has bin
>   In every Heart since *Adams* sin,
> I'll lay my *Life*, nay *Mistress* on't, that's more;
> I'll teach him things he never knew before;
>   I'll teach him a *Receipt* to make
>   *Words* that *weep*, and *Tears* that *speak*,
>   I'll teach him *Sighs*, like those in *Death*.
> At which the *Souls* go out too with the breath;
> Still the *Soul stays*, yet still does from me *run*;
>   As *Light* and *Heat* does with the *Sun*.
>
> 'Tis I who *Love's Columbus* am: 'tis I,
>   Who must new *Worlds* in it descry:
>   Rich *Worlds*, that yield of *Treasure* more,
>   Than all that has bin known before.
> And yet like *his* (I fear) my *Fate* must be,
> To find them out for *others*; not for *Me*.
>   Me Times to come, I know it, shall
>   Loves last and greatest *Prophet* call.
>   But, ah, what's that, if she refuse,
> To hear the wholesome *Doctrines* of my *Muse*?
> If to my share the *prophets fate* must come;
>   Hereafter *Fame*, here *Martyrdome*.[27]

Beautifully modulated, the poem introduces Cowley's use of
religious imagery in love lyrics and allies him with Donne and
those martyrs *"canoniz'd"* for Love." The great irony lies in the

reader's awareness that the speaker seems to know little of love itself but a great deal of love's literary traditions.

The Mistress was immediately a popular collection, but its popularity has decreased ever since. Dryden's critical questions in 1693 marked the beginning of the end. Donne "affects the metaphysics," Dryden wrote,

> not only in his satires, but in his amorous verses, where nature only should reign; and perplexes the minds of the fair sex with nice speculations of philosophy, when he should engage their hearts, and entertain them with the softnesses of love. In this (if I may be pardoned for so bold a truth) Mr. Cowley has copied him to a fault; so great a one, in my opinion, that it throws his *Mistress* infinitely below his Pindarics, and his latter compositions, which are undoubtedly the best of his poems, and the most correct.[28]

Love poems ought to set out to win the lady, Dryden thought, not lecture her on the dilemmas of passion.[29] For Cowley, love was an occasion to write witty poems to impress the reader with his own versatility. Johnson's comments, justly famous, begin by echoing those of Dryden: "But, considered as the verses of a lover, no man that has ever loved will much commend them. They are neither courtly nor pathetick, have neither gallantry nor fondness. His praises are too far sought and too hyperbolical, either to express love or to excite it: every stanza is crouded with darts and flames, with wounds and death, with mingled souls, and with broken hearts."

The unkindest cut of all concludes Johnson's account: "Cowley's *Mistress* has no power of seduction; she 'plays round the head, but comes not at the heart.' Her beauty and absence, her kindness and cruelty, her disdain and inconstancy, produce no correspondence of emotion. His poetical account of the virtues of plants and colours of flowers is not perused with more sluggish frigidity. The compositions are such as might have been written for penance by a hermit, or for hire by a philosophical rhymer who had only heard of another sex."[30] For Edmund Gosse, the poems are dull and metrically inept, "unreadable . . . dry and tedious, without tenderness, without melancholy, without music."[31] Modern criticism has dealt no less harshly with the lyrics that so fascinated contemporary audiences.[32]

There seems little reason to question the generally unfavorable opinion of *The Mistress,* but one ought to remember that, though

Cowley may be little more than a brilliant imitator of John Donne, that in itself is an achievement. Since Donne in many of his poems is not at all the serious wooer but the courtier playing in love, readers ought also to consider that Cowley in some of his lyrics at least is also playing in love. Many of the great successes of *The Mistress*—poems like *"Platonick Love," "Written in Juice of Lemon," "The Soul,"* and *"The Prophet"*—contain elements which not long before Cowley had categorized as false wit in his *"Ode. Of Wit."* One also notices these charactcristics when he reads Donne's poems, but Donne often has the true wit to bring those verbal flashes under control.

In some of the best poems from the group Cowley may be satirizing the vogue for Donne's mannerisms. He is not serious about love at all, but he is serious about technique in love verses. If intellectual hardness was in vogue, then he would have that; if metaphors with religious terms were popular, he would use them; if figures from politics were a mark of the new style, he could invent with the best. Sometimes the results were fortunate, but too often one is confronted with poems that bore him. There are too many poor products to suggest the defense that they are all *exempla* of false wit.[33]

Self-mockery, nevertheless, is not uncommon in poetry; and Cecily Wedgwood has been quite perceptive about that tendency in the seventeenth century:

Insulated by the calm assurance of the eighteenth century, Johnson makes mock of Cleveland's elaborate verses on, for instance, the black sunshine imprisoned in the Newcastle coal mines. But he is mocking unseasonably, for Cleveland himself is not serious; there is an undercurrent of self-mockery, of mock-heroic (or should it be mock-metaphysical?) in nearly all these poets, when Lovelace, describing the battle of Lepanto, marries the sublime to the ridiculous with his "And the sick sea with turbans night-capp'd was," he expects to raise a smile. Lovelace again has been attacked because, in *Lucasta Weeping*, his mistress, by a fantastic metaphor, has her tears wiped from her cheek by "the soft hankercher of light"—dried by the sun, in fact; but this is mock-metaphysical again, a deliberate showing off on his part: "Look what a quaint conceit I have here." For those who are deaf to these undertones of self-mockery in the lighter metaphysical poets (Lovelace, Cleveland, and Cowley in particular) much of this verse must necessarily seem offensive and absurd.[34]

If Cowley frequently mocked current tendencies, it must have delighted him to play wittily with the fancies of his age. The relationships with Donne, then, become very important; for what Cowley has done is to catch the surface brilliance but not the passion or depth revealed in the arguments of a Donne poem. Cowley's lover is deliberately distant; what lover, he asks, can argue philosophically and rationally and be passionately involved with his lady at the same moment? And Cowley's lady is deliberately a phantom, for in his poems the speaker becomes the central figure. The occasion is his to inflate his ego and to satisfy others as to his ingenuity. Donne challenged the ingenuity of wits in love poetry; Cowley picked up the challenge and offered examples of the mock-metaphysical in Donne's mode.

CHAPTER 4

"*The* Phoenix Pindar"

I "*Pindarique Pegasus*"

F ROM the outrageous extravagances of the love lyrics, one turns to the formal, ceremonial odes in the "stile and manner" of Pindar. Cowley began these "hymns" (which were chiefly responsible for his continued popularity)[1] after an "accidental meeting with *Pindars* Works in a place where he had no other Books to direct him."[2] His leisurely experiments in free versification on the barren Isle of Jersey were to introduce the way of Pindar to England.[3] When the odes were eventually published, Cowley was "in great doubt" whether his tentative excursions in the form would be "understood by most *Readers*." The long and sudden digressions, bold figures, irregular numbers, and the seemingly random cadances took great liberty with traditional patterns; but, as Sprat observed, we may be "tyr'd by the setled pace of any one constant measure,"[4] and, besides, the boldness was Pindar's and not Cowley's.

Cowley knew that Pindar's verses maintained a formal regularity,[5] but it was not his intention to provide a "metaphrase" ("turning an author word by word and line by line, from one language into another"); instead, his objective was an "imitation," where "the translator (if now he has not lost that name) assumes the liberty not only to vary from the words and sense, but to forsake them both as he sees occasion; and taking only some general hints from the original, to run division on the ground-work, as he pleases."[6] He thought that freedom especially necessary in the case of Pindar, whose metaphors were frequently distant and difficult to follow; "if a man should undertake to translate *Pindar* word for word," he wrote, "it would be thought that one *Mad man* had translated *another*."[7]

The reader ought to "consider in *Pindar* the great difference of time betwixt his age and ours, which changes, as in *Pictures*,

at least the *Colours* of *Poetry,* the no less difference betwixt the
Religious and *Customs* of our Countrys, and a thousand par-
ticularities of places, persons, and manners, which do but
confusedly appear to our Eyes at so great a distance."[8] Liberty
to vary the original is also dangerous, and Dryden warned that
such license should be given only to men of Cowley's genius:

> To add and to diminish what we please, which is the way avowed
> by him [Denham], ought only to be granted to Mr. Cowley, and
> that too only in his translation of Pindar, because he alone was able
> to make him amends, by giving him better of his own whenever he
> refused his author's thoughts. Pindar is generally known to be a dark
> writer, to want connection (I mean as to our understanding), to soar
> out of sight, and leave his reader at a gaze. So wild and ungovernable
> a poet cannot be translated literally, his genius is too strong to bear a
> chain, and Samson-like he shakes it off. A genius so elevated and
> unconfined as Mr. Cowley's was but necessary to make Pindar speak
> English, and that was to be performed by no other way than
> imitation.[9]

It was a bold venture to translate the Pindarics, and it would take,
Dryden thought, bolder men to equal Cowley's achievement.

The first two odes in the group, the Second Olympic and the
First Nemean, are Cowleyan imitations of Pindaric victory
songs: one is in praise of Theron of Agrigentum; the other, in
honor of Chromius of Sicily. Cowley thought of them as intro-
ductory "essays" in the form, and they were to let his readers
know the *"way* and *manner"* of Pindar's speaking.[10] For instance,
Theron's song *"consists more in* Digressions," Cowley informs
his readers, *"than in the main* subject"; but those digressions are
closely ordered. Moving quickly from the present into the past,
the song celebrates Theron's ancestry and chronicles the family
history and its fortunes. From the past, the ode looks to the
future and the eternal joys of fortunate men in Hades, "land of
unexhausted *Light."* Following the formal and ceremonial begin-
ning, seven of the nine stanzas have moved the reader further
away from the present moment; in stanza nine, Cowley stops to
survey the course of Pindar's poem:

> To *Theron, Muse,* bring back thy wondring Song,
> Whom those bright Troops expect impatiently;
>   And may they do so long.
> How, nobler *Archer,* do thy wanton *Arrows* fly

At all the *Game* that does but cross thine Eye?
    Shoot, and spare not, for I see
The sounding *Quiver* can ne're emptied be;
Let *Art* use *Method* and good *Husbandry*,
Art lives on *Natures Alms*, is weak and poor;
Nature herself has unexhausted store,
Wallows in *Wealth*, and runs a turning *Maze*,
    That no *vulgar Eye* can trace.
Art instead of mounting high,
About her *humble Food* does hov'ering fly,
Like the ignoble *Crow, rapine,* and *noise* does love,
Whilst *Nature,* like the sacred *Bird* of *Jove,*
Now bears loud *Thunder,* and anon with *silent joy*
    The beauteous *Phrygian Boy,*
Defeats the *Strong,* o'retakes the *Flying* prey;
And sometimes basks in th'open *Flames* of *Day,*
    And sometimes too he shrouds,
    His soaring *wings* among the *Clouds.*[11]

Cowley's note reveals his awareness that "the Connexion in the *Poet* is very obscure,"[12] but the metaphor of arrows and quivers is a Pindaric favorite. The poet is an archer whose "wanton *Arrows*" (creative impulses) fly out at every target (subject) that passes. Art, however, always weak and poor compared with nature, stays like "the ignoble *Crow*," close to earth; nature, in its abundance, soars in the air sacred to Jove (Pindar, Cowley warns, loves to speak of his own Muse in his poems.)[13] This recapitulation is one way to describe what is happening in the poem; and, while this summation implies a greater sense of random selection than is actually the case, it also reveals that Cowley is well aware of the degree of enthusiasm the variety of movement conveys. In the two concluding stanzas the ode resumes its figure from archery to eulogize Theron and his accomplishments:

Leave, wanton *Muse,* thy roving flight,
To thy loud *String* the well-fletcht *Arrow* put,
    Let [A] *grigentum* be the *But,*
    And *Theron* be the *White.*[14]

Preparatory work on the two imitations led to another experiment: Cowley's abridged version of Horace's Second Ode (Book IV) on Pindar ("Pindarum quisquis studet aemulari")[15] which is characterized by its audacious "soaring" from one topic to another. The result is that Pindar's songs appear, in Cowley's fine metaphor, "unnavigable"—capable of drowning "any *Head* that is not strong built and well *ballasted*."[16] Pindar's enthusiastic rage overcomes the roar of the sea, while the voices of lesser followers perish in the waters:

> *Pindar* is imitable by none,
>> The *Phoenix Pindar* is a vast *Species alone.*
> Who e're but *Daedalus* with waxen wings could fly
> And neither *sink* too low, nor *soar* too high?
>> What could he who *follow'd* claim,
> But of vain *boldness* the unhappy fame,
>> And by his fall a Sea to name?
>> *Pindars unnavigable Song*
> Like a swoln *Flood* from some steep *Mountain* pours along,
>> The Ocean meets with such a *Voice*
> From his enlarged *Mouth,* as drowns the *Oceans* noise.[17]

The wild but controlled impetuousness of Pindar never fails to dazzle, for what readers admire in his "*Dithyrambique Tide*" is its freedom, its "lawless measures," its passion to include all things within its frenzied flood:

> So *Pindar* does now *Words* and *Figures* roul
> Down his impetuous *Dithyrambique Tide,*
>> Which in no *Channel* deigns t'abide,
>> Which neither *Banks* nor *Dikes* controul.
>> Whether th'*Immortal Gods he sings*
>> In a no less *Immortal strain,*
> Or the great Acts of *God-descended Kings*
> Who in his Numbers still survive and *Reign.*
>> Each rich embroidered *Line,*
>> Which their triumphant *Brows* around,
>> By his sacred Hand is bound,
> Does all their *starry Diadems* outshine.
> Whether at *Pisa's* race he please,
> To *carve* in polisht *Verse* the *Conque'rors Images,*
> Whether the *Swift,* the *Skilful,* or the *Strong,*
> Be crowned in his *Nimble, Artful, Vigorous Song*:
> Whether some brave young man's untimely fate
> In words worth *Dying for* he celebrate,
>> Such *mournful,* and such *pleasing* words,
> As *joy* to'his *Mothers* and his *Mistress grief* affords:

> He bids him *Live* and *Grow* in fame,
>   Among the *Stars* he sticks his *Name*:
> The *Grave* can but the *Dross* of him devour,
> So *small* is *Deaths,* so *great* the *Poets* power.[18]

Cowley's final stanza echoes the opening images of flight, and Pindar is the *"Theban Swan"* carried high into the air; Cowley's *"tim'erous Muse"* (like Horace's) is content with humbler, domestic "flights." But these "lesser flights" are made to seem all the more important and significant—all the more believable—when compared with the fantastic abilities of Pindar. There are more humble things to be sung, and there are always the celebrators of the commonplaces whose magic is performed on gardens and fields:

> Lo, how th'obsequious *Wind,* and swelling Ayr
>   The *Theban Swan* does upwards bear
> Into the *walks* of *Clouds,* where he does play,
> And with extended *Wings* opens his liquid way.
>   Whilst, alas, my *tim'erous Muse*
>   *Unambitious* tracks pursues;
>   Does with weak unballast wings
>   About the *mossy Brooks* and *Springs*;
>   About the *Trees* new-blossom'ed *Heads,*
>   About the *Gardens* painted *Beds,*
>   About the *Fields* and flowry *Meads,*
>   And all *inferior beauteous things*
>   Like the laborious *Bee,*
>   For little drops of *Honey* flee,
> And there with *Humble Sweets* contents her *Industrie.*[19]

The poem modulates beautifully here, and it concludes with the favorite Alexandrine.

II   *"My Tim'erous Muse"*

Three of the Cowley odes—*"The Resurrection," "The Muse,"* and *"To Mr.* Hobs"—are concerned with the function of poetry and the roles of poet and philosopher. *"The Resurrection,"* "truly *Pindarical,* falling from one thing into another, after his *Enthusiastical manner* . . . ,"[20] considers first the special role of poetry in the universe. Until the day of final judgment, the years "decently advance" in dance to the poet's music; when the great trumpets sound, however, poets are powerless to sing. Until that time, poetry has assured an orderly progression of earthly events, for its functions as the divine representative. Cowley concludes his ode suddenly; his muse, he complains playfully, is all too fond of dashing headlong into a subject and carrying its rider away:

> Stop, stop, my *Muse*, allay thy vig'orous heat,
>> Kindled at a *Hint* so Great.
> Hold thy *Pindarique Pegasus* closely in,
>> Which does to *rage* begin,
> And this steep *Hill* would gallop up with violent course,
> 'Tis an unruly, and a *hard-Mouth'd Horse*,
>> Fierce, and unbroken yet,
>> Impatient of the *Spur* and *Bit*.
> Now *praunces* stately, and anon flies o're the place,
> Disdains the *servile Law* of any setled *pace*,
> *Conscious* and *proud* of his own *natural force*.
>> 'Twill no *unskilful Touch* endure,
> But flings *Writer* and *Reader* too that *sits* not *sure*.[21]

The notes to "*The Muse*" reveal as much as the poem does about Cowley's attitudes toward poetry. "All things must be," he had written, in a work of true wit, where the poet's art organizes everything so all is "heightened" but nothing is changed. This notion appears again in the couplet: "Whatever *God* did *Say*, / Is all thy plain and smooth, uninterrupted *way*."[22] Poetry makes its own worlds, and the poetic act has its analogy in God's act of creation:

Whatsoever God made, for his saying, *Let it be*, made all things. The meaning is, that *Poetry* treats not only of all things that are, or can be, but makes *Creatures* of her own, as *Centaurs, Satyrs, Faires*, &c. makes *persons* and *actions* of her own, as in *Fables* and *Romances*, makes *Beasts, Trees, Waters*, and other irrational and insensible things to act above the possibility of their natures, as to *understand* and *speak*, nay makes what *Gods* it pleases too with *Idolatry*, and varies all these into innumerable *Systemes*, or *Worlds* of Invention.[23]

And, as Pindar has illustrated in his Second Olympic by fusing past, present, and future into a logical whole, "The subject of *Poetry* is all *Past, Future* and *Present Times*; and for the Past, it makes what choice it pleases out of the *wrack* of *Time* of things that it will have from *Oblivion*."[24]

Actually, *"The Muse"* is a poem about the creative process; and its significance as a statement is greater than its value as a poem. For Cowley, poetic creation involves all human faculties—fancy, judgment, wit, invention, memory, and eloquence—each paired with its complementary characteristic. In a chariot conceit, the poem's basic figure, the muse prepares to "take the air," and her team is harnessed; memory, passive in nature, is given life by the strength of invention; "nimble-footed *Wit*" is kept within the bounds of decorum by eloquence; and fancy's airy ramblings are given substance by judgment. *"Figures, Conceits, Raptures,* and *Sentences"* act as footmen, while Art, the great coachman, is watched over by the postilion, Nature. The poetic nature prepares to soar forth; and the past, present, and future are all an open road. The poet's choice of subject is unlimited.

Having discussed the past and noticed the future in a bold metaphor of an embryo forming within the shell, the ode concludes with an important statement about what poetry does with the present:

> And sure we may
> The same too of the *Present* say,
> If *Past,* and *Future Times* do thee obey.
> Thou stopst this *Current,* and dost make
> This running *River* settle like a *Lake,*
> Thy certain hand holds fast this slippery *Snake.*
> The *Fruit* which does so quickly wast,
> Men scarce can see it, must less *tast,*
> Thou *Comfitest* in *Sweets* to make it *last.*
> This shining piece of *Ice*
> Which melts so soon away
> With the *Suns* ray,
> Thy *Verse* does solidate and *Chrystallize,*
> Till it a lasting *Mirror* be.
> Nay thy *Immortal Rhyme*
> Makes this one short *Point* of *Time,*
> To fill up half the *Orb* of *Round Eternity.*[25]

Poetry is an image of the eternal; whatever it handles that is temporal and transitory, it "solidate[s] and *Chrystalize*[s]." In the scientific image, whatever natural power creates poetry is that mysterious force which makes crystals out of a fluid substance. The crystals, the poems, are examples of nature herself isolated, heightened, and dramatized. "The poet," writes Robert Hinman, "needs the phenomena of the physical world to perform his exalted function."[26] No one concentrated more on those observable phenomena than Cowley's associate, Thomas Hobbes, the subject of an ode whose topics are extensions of those in "*The Muse.*"

The imagination of Cowley's poet dealt with all creation, and he found the nearest counterpart to that artistic strength in the philosopher Thomas Hobbes, the "great *Columbus* of the *Golden Lands* of *new Philosophies.*" Nowhere in Cowley's ode does one find anything except praise, but attacks on Hobbes by others were violent accusations of atheism.[27] Cowley thought of Hobbes as the great philosopher-poet whose investigations led to ultimate natural truths about the state of man. Hobbes had discovered a new set of analogies between God and the universe, man and his commonwealth, the soul and the body; and his genius, eloquence, and wit had "*planted, peopled, built*, and *civiliz'd*" his discovery. It had been given artful form, logically ordered, proportioned, and presented "full of concord":

> I little thought before
> (Nor being my *own self* so *poor*
> Could comprehend so vast a *store*)
> That all the *Wardrobe* of rich *Eloquence*,
> Could have afforded half enuff,
> Of *bright*, of *new*, and *lasting* stuff,
> To cloath the mighty *Limbs* of thy *Gigantique Sence*.
> Thy solid *Reason* like the *shield* from heaven
> To the *Trojan Heroe* given,
> Too strong to take a mark from any mortal dart,
> Yet shines with *Gold* and *Gems* in every part,
> And *Wonders* on it grave'd by the learn'd hand of *Art*,
> A *shield* that gives delight
> Even to the *enemies* sight,
> Then when they're sure to *lose* the Combat by't.[28]

The beauty of Hobbes's form dazzles his antagonists, for the "poetry of philosophy" had in its defense a modern and more powerful version of Aeneas's shield (Reason), upon which it newly engraved all that need be known of human history. Having discovered not only the basic order at the heart of the universe through the observance of natural phenomena, Hobbes has imaged that order in his work, itself the artistic analogy of the philosophic truth. It is not difficult to see why Cowley, a poet who sought to present an imaged order of all things, should give to the mind and discoveries of Thomas Hobbes the emphasis he does. To be a good philosopher was also to be a good poet.[29]

The year 1655 was not only the date of "To Mr. Hobs" but also of "Brutus" and "To Dr. Scarborough." That was the year of Cowley's imprisonment, and two of the odes may be conciliatory offerings. Hobbes had made his peace with Oliver Cromwell early in 1651, and "Brutus" (without the extensive prose commentary which accompanies the other odes) may be an invitation to consider classical parallels between Rome and England, Caesar and Charles, Brutus and Cromwell. To an age embroiled in civil controversy and accustomed to political allegory, the correspondences were probably obvious. Brutus is characterized through a circle image; around his virtue all parts move in order and proportion. Such a man could commit no imperfection, although the moral powers of men sometimes clouded their understanding of the true nature of his acts. But no virtuous man could stand by and see his country ravished and remain inactive:

> Can we stand by and see
> Our *Mother* robb'ed, and bound, and ravisht be,
> Yet not to her assistance stir,
> Pleas'd with the *Strength* and *Beauty* of the *Ravisher*?
> Or shall we fear to kill him, if before
> The *cancell'd Name* of *Friend* he bore?
> *Ingrateful Brutus* do they call?
> *Ingrateful Caesar* who could *Rome* enthrall!
> An act more barbarous and unnatural
> (In th'exact ballance of true *Virtue* try'de)
> Then his *Successor Nero's Parricide!*
> There's none but *Brutus* could deserve
> That all men else should *wish* to *serve*,
> And *Caesars* usurpt place to him should proffer;
> None can deserve't but he who would *refuse* the *offer*.[30]

Had Brutus lived only a few more years, he would have seen the birth of Christianity and a new set of standards given the world by a man misunderstood and put to death by his own people. Brutus, a predecessor of the Christ, suggests Cromwell as his modern counterpart. If England will support her idealistic leader, she too will experience a rebirth. This occasional ode reveals Cowley's passionate support of Cromwell's government; more relevant to the poet's work generally, however, is the ode to his benefactor, Dr. Charles Scarborough.

Like Hobbes, who, observing natural phenomena, discovered "natural man," Scarborough "know'st all so well that's done within, / As if some *living Chrystal Man* thou'dst seem." And like Hobbes, his specialized knowledge did not preclude the gentle arts, for the reader is reminded that *"Apollo* is not only the *God* of *Physick,* but of *Poetry,* and all kind of *Florid Learning."*[31] Scarborough, then, has double cause to be praised; he is that rare physician not suffering from *"Fantastick Incivilitie"* who is also a man of letters. The ode again reveals Cowley's interest in the scientific experiments carried on by men like Boyle and Harvey and by those who were later to form the Royal Society.

In a nice hyperbole which opens the poem, Cowley claims that "the *Ruines* of a *Civil War"* (in body and in body politic) are repaired by Scarborough, a man familiar with "the vast and barbarous *Lexicon* / Of Mans *Infirmitie."* Scarborough appears another of those human beings whose actions were responsible for saving a nation bent on suicide in civil war. Whatever oppressors which pervert the orderly course of nature—*"Inundations* of all *Liquid pain,"* the "subtle *Ague,"* *"Deluge Dropsie,"* or the "cruel *Stone"*—are defeated and controlled by the depth of Scarborough's knowledge, one so comprehensive it reaches from earth to heaven and peers into the secrets of both:

> From creeping *Moss* to soaring *Cedar* thou
> Dost all the powers and several *Portions* know
> Which *Father-Sun, Mother-Earth* below
>   On their green *Infants* here bestow.
> Can'st all those *Magick Virtues* from them draw,
>   That keep *Disease,* and *Death* in aw.
> Who whilst thy wondrous skill in *Plants* they see,
> Fear lest the *Tree of Life* should be found out by Thee.
> And Thy well-travell'd knowledge too does give
> No less account of th'*Empire Sensitive.*
>   Chiefly of *Man,* whose *Body* is

That active *Souls Metropolis.*
As the great Artist in his *Sphere* of *Glass*
Saw the whole *Scene* of Heav'enly *Motions* pass,
So thou know'st all so well that's done within,
As if some *living Chrystal Man* thou'dst seen.[32]

Having discovered the *"Magick Virtues"* inherent in the world
of nature, Scarborough may soon discover also the secret of
existence, sharply metaphorized by Cowley as "the *Tree of
Life.*" And, like Hobbes's, Scarborough's knowledge is synthetic;
he works by verifying order in the physical world and then
applying that knowledge to its nearest analogy, the world of
men. In turn, the "order" seen in men is analogous to those
"Heaven'ly *Motions*" seen by the "great Artist." But part of the
order to which all men are subject is mortality, and no matter
how one may wish to change Hippocrites's aphorism, "Ars
longa, vita brevis," to offer a deserved compliment, "When all's
done, *Life is an Incurable Disease.*" With this maxim, Cowley
closes his hymn to Scarborough, having given him the highest
praise possible by grouping his name with those intellects who
discover and preserve universal order.

The only regular stanzaic ode in the group is "The Extasie."[33]
In this ode Cowley sees himself as the "Columbus" of the cos-
mos, an image he had used to describe Hobbes and Scarborough.
In vision, the poet wings his way into the heavens to view the
secrets there. Exhilarated as he passes the ordered cosmos
through the clouds into a sea of flame beyond the "several *Orbs*
which one fair *Planet* bear," he moves into the empyrean bright-
ness, an "unexhausted *Ocean* of *delight*," inhabited by God and
angels. Here Elijah was also destined; and, like Elijah and
Hobbes and Scarborough, Cowley is also the prophet of order
and harmony; "The Extasie" records his vision of world unity
and numbers him among poets and philosophers with a prophetic
mission.

The next group of Pindarics—*"Destinie," "Life and Fame,"
"To the New Year,"* and *"Life"*—extends the range of subject
matter and contemplates the nature of life and existence. *"Des-
tinie"* opens with a metaphor from chess: "the extravagant sup-
position of two *Angels* playing a *Game* at *Chess.*"[34] Extending
the figure to include men as the pawns of destiny, Cowley reviews
his whole life in these terms: his was a life he did not choose;

instead, it chose him. His fate was to renounce all worldly treasure, to be great in no great enterprise, to be content with "the small *Barren Praise,* / That neglected *Verse* does raise." Almost joyously he accepts his position in life, and with small modesty and no little pride he concludes:

> With *Fate* what boots it to contend?
> Such I *began,* such *am,* and so must *end.*
> The *Star* that did my *Being* frame,
> Was but a *Lambent Flame,*
> And some small *Light* it did dispence,
> But neither *Heat* nor *Influence.*
> No Matter, *Cowley,* let proud *Fortune* see,
> That *thou* canst *her* despise no less then *she* does *Thee.*
> Let all her gifts the portion be
> Of Folly, Lust, and Flattery,
> Fraud, Extortion, Calumnie,
> Murder, Infidelitie,
> Rebellion and Hypocrisie.
> Do Thou nor *grieve* nor *blush* to be,
> As all th'inspired *tuneful Men,*
> And all thy great *Forefathers* were from *Homer* down to *Ben.*[35]

There is, however, much pessimism in these poems, partly perhaps the result of Cowley's imprisonment and partly a general disillusionment with the state of the civil commonwealth. In "*Life and Fame,*" existence for him is only a shadow, an isthmus between past and future, a dream some men attempt to perpetuate; of the perpetuators, poets are the maddest of all, those who "with a refin'ed *Phantastick Vanitie,* / Think we not onely *Have,* but *Give Eternitie.*"[36] With equal resignation he contemplates the passage of time and the arrival of a new cycle in "*To the New Year.*" No one need celebrate the new year nor attempt to foresee what it brings, for "the *Book* of *Fate* is writ." Those shivering souls standing on the brink of the new year suffer least who "plunge" into it quickly:

> Upon the *Brink* of every *Ill* we did *Foresee,*
> Undecently and foolishlie
> We should stand *shivering,* and but slowly venter
> The *Fatal Flood* to enter,
> Since *willing,* or *unwilling,* we must do it,
> They feel least *cold* and *pain* who *plunge* at once into it.[37]

Some of the same pessimism is echoed in *"Life"* (the epigraph is *"Nacentes Morimur"*), in which life is described as a *"Transparent Fallacie"* seen through only by prophets. Life, he says, is simply an inn, a step, and not the whole race. Man's artful maintenance of this "temporary" condition (responsible for all his sufferings) succeeds only in imprisoning the "noble vigorous *Bird*" (the soul) in "death" when it wishes only to fly away to "life."

The day of judgment, the end of this vanity and folly which men consider life, is described in Cowley's version of "The 34. Chapter of the Prophet *Isaiah*." Isaiah's prophecy deals specifically with the destruction of Judea, but his method illustrates "these confusions by the similitude of them to those of the last Day, though in the Text there would be no Transition from the *subject* to the *similitude*."[38] Isaiah's method appealed to Cowley, for he succeeded in universalizing his local and national subject matter through an implicit parallel to the day of judgment. And, equally as important, "the manner of the *Prophets* writing, especially of *Isaiah*, seems to me very like that of *Pindar*; they pass from one thing to another with almost *Invisible connexions*, and are full of words and expressions of the highest and boldest flights of *Poetry*, as may be seen in this Chapter, where there are as extraordinary Figures as can be found in any *Poet* whatsoever; and the connexion is so difficult, that I am forced to adde a little, and leave out a great deal, to make it seem *Sense* to us, who are not used to that elevated way of expression."[39]

What Cowley has done is to give the account the logical unity and order which would have been apparent to a contemporary reader of the original but which would not be apparent in a literal translation. The unifying metaphor is earth as God's sacrifice; as man has for centuries slaughtered animals, so now God will make man His victim and earth His altar. Destroying angels follow to make sure no one is left alive, and the world is turned over to the animals. What Cowley's version has accomplished is the successful fusion of the particular with the universal to give the subject heightened grandeur and nobility, and one guesses that the ode is a warning to his own time.

The last of the Pindarics in the section is the virtuoso performance *"The Plagues of* Egypt." Nineteen long, irregular stanzas support a melodrama heavily laden with all kinds of Classical and biblical learning. The story of Moses and the

Pharaoh is a horrifying exemplum to those who would ignore
God's wonders and his love. Cataloguing the plagues and ex-
panding stanzas to dramatize the horrors brought on by Pharaoh's
disbelief, Cowley reveals that he has obviously mastered the
form as he conceived it. The infinite variations in line length
give the reader an impression of significant differences in each
stanza, and this freedom allows Cowley to compress or to expand
an image or metaphor within a given stanza as the logic of the
line or stanza dictates at the moment. In spite of its length and
the dangers of repetition inherent in the subject itself—or of a
fatal evenness in narrative progression—the poem maintains its
narrative excitement in passages like the following:

> As gentle western Blasts with downy wings
> Hatching the tender *Springs,*
> To th'unborn *Buds* with vital whispers say,
> Ye *living Buds* why do ye stay?
> The passionate *Buds* break through the *Bark* their way:
> So wheresoere this *tainted Wind* but blew,
> Swelling *pains* and *Ulcers* grew;
> It from the body call'ed all *sleeping Poysons* out,
> And to them added new;
> A noysome *Spring* of *Sores,* as thick as *Leaves* did sprout.[40]

The breath of God inspiring the birth of buds and plants is the
ironic counterpart to this macabre, death-giving wind which
prompts the births of malignancies and distortions.

Cowley never stopped writing Pindaric odes (there are several
examples in his occasional verses of 1663), and his contemporary
reputation was based exclusively upon them. The odes are
literary set pieces, ceremonial hymns in which a human subject
can be given eternal and cosmic significance; as such, they
satisfied his era's love of the grandiose and the magnificent. The
ode is, as Geoffrey Walton reminds us, "a parallel phenomenon
to the heroic play."[41] The odes stand midway between the
exclusively witty performances of *The Mistress* and the stately
and high seriousness of the *Davideis*; lyric and epic meet in the
ode, the seventeenth- and eighteenth-century counterpart to the
Renaissance sonnet sequence. The form itself admits an infinite
variation in rhyme scheme, line, and stanza length; each instance
is an opportunity for the virtuoso to startle and please his audi-
ence with boldness and novelty.

And Pindar's penchant for speaking of his muse—the ease
with which the poet could suddenly bring the problems of art
and nature into the poem itself—offered Cowley significant op-
portunities to formulate and comment upon his own poetics.
Cowley's audience was undoubtedly excited by the wit and
ingenuity of a poet who could sustain such productions and con-
stantly convey that *"furor poeticus,"* soaring on the wings of
inspiration oblivious of traditional patterns and depending only
upon his individual talent. Cowley and his concept of creation
in a frenzy endeared him to his own time; ironically, one thinks
of him as a poet whose enduring temper was that of the Horatian
Bee rather than the Theban Swan.

CHAPTER 5

"I sing the Man *who* Judah's Scepter *bore"*

I *Mortal Wit and Heavenly Truths*

COWLEY'S century praised his *Davideis* as a poem greater than the epics of Tasso, Spenser, and Milton. Dryden admired it, and, in 1667, the year of the publication of *Paradise Lost,* Samuel Woodford found in the *Davideis* as "much as could be expected for the first sitting . . . whatever is requisite to make an heroick poem beautiful: sound judgment, happy invention, graceful disposition, unaffected facility, strict observation of decencies. . . ."[1] In his "Preface to the Translation of Rapin's *Reflections on Aristotle's Treatise of Poesie*" (1674), Thomas Rhymer also praised the poem:

A more happy *Genius* for *Heroick Poesie* appears in *Cowley.* He understood the *purity,* the *perspicuity,* the *majesty* of stile and the vertue of *numbers.* He could discern what was beautiful and pleasant in Nature, and could express his Thoughts without the least difficulty of restraint. He understood to dispose of the matters, and to manage his Digressions. In short, he understood *Homer* and *Virgil,* and as prudently made his advantage of them.[2]

In 1693, Samuel Wesley considered the *Davideis* a "medium" between *Gondibert* and *The Faerie Queene:* "it has Gondibert's Majesty without his stiffness, and something of Spencer's Sweetness and Variety without his Irregularity."[3] The great panegyric on the poem, however, will always be Thomas Sprat's, who, thinking Cowley had written the epic while still a young man, conceded that "there may have been more youthfulness and redundance of Fancy than his riper judgment would have allowed"; still Sprat's praise is hyperbole:

The main of it, I will affirm, that it is a better instance and beginning of a Divine Poem than I ever yet saw in any Language. The contrivance is perfectly ancient, which is certainly the true form of Heroick Poetry, and such as was never yet outdone by any new

Devices of Modern Wits. The subject was truly Divine, even according to Gods own heart: The matter of his invention, all the Treasures of Knowledge and Histories in the Bible. The model of it comprehended all the Learning of the East: The Characters, lofty and various; The Numbers, firm and powerful; The Digressions, beautiful and proportionable; The Design, to submit mortal Wit to heavenly Truths: in all there is an admirable mixture of humane Virtues and Passions with religious Raptures.[4]

Few in the seventeenth century had unkind words for the *Davideis,* but modern opinions of the epic almost unanimously contradict the earlier ones. The often sympathetic Edmund Gosse thought the first book had some virtues, but "the other three books of this epic are tedious and redundant beyond all endurance. It is, in fact, the sort of poem with which, if you sit on the grass in a quiet place some summer afternoon, you cannot by any means fail to slumber soundly. This is indeed its only merit, save that of marking a distinct step in the process of the ossification of the English heroic couplet."[5]

Loiseau recognized its shortcomings in Cowley's ineffectual reconciliation of the old and new; Robert Hinman is one of few for whom the poem is "worth reading," primarily as a valuable record of Cowley's interest in science and of scientific concepts in the seventeenth century. Miltonists are generally the harshest critics: B. Rajan calls attention to Cowley's "dismal performance" in comparison to Milton's brilliant epic,[6] and Cecily Wedgwood is hardly less severe with her references to Cowley's "lovely lines" which are "all, somehow, too light and watery for the majestic Biblical subject."[7] The tone of the account given by Douglas Bush conveys the archetypal modern opinion of the poem:

Bits of nature and Oriental life and of psychological analysis, and the ideal friendship of David and Jonathan which appealed to Dorothy Osborne, are not enough to give life to "the Cold-meats of the Antients," and we are more attracted, as the poet was, by such peripheral matters of topical and philosophic interest as the ideal college and the question of monarchy or republic, physical phenomena and metaphysics. Though aware of modern views and of "endless space," Cowley accepts the Ptolemaic system for his Hebrew story, and his cosmology is a mixture of old and new, of Neoplatonism and science. The world was created "From Nothing," by the triune God of Christianity, who with His angels combats Lucifer and his demons. The primal elements ranged themselves in order under the compulsion of Music and Love. The universe is "God's Poem," "the aeternal Minds Poetick Thought." It is also "Great Natures well-set Clock," but a clock which, "the Schoolmen all agree" (if not the law of inertia), requires the "immediate concurse of God." But, despite Cowley's broad horizons, his combination of traditional religious and Platonic thought with scientific modernism, he had neither the intellectual nor the poetic power for such a synthesis of science and imagination as the divided age was in need of.[8]

Bush's view seemingly owes its debt to Johnson's life of Cowley.

Johnson's balanced estimate of the unfinished *Davideis* is a dramatic instance of his fairness in dealing with Cowley. The discussion is a long one, for Johnson was aware how few critics and readers had said anything about the epic; what praise they did confer upon Cowley's other works they intended for the *Davideis* as well. Johnson' critique is divided into matters of subject and of style. His first topics (one sees them again in his discussion of Milton) are the problems of poetic decorum and the divine subject and the difficulties in achieving any sort of empathy on the reader's part for things beyond his scope, ability, and imagination (the character of God). From such questions Johnson moves to epic style, where he is critical of the excesses of Cowley's conceits; the major stylistic weakness of the *Davideis,* he thought, was that it is "narrative spangled with conceits." Cowley offends both by diminution and exaggeration; Johnson's example, "the dress of Gabriel," is well chosen:

> He took for skin a cloud most soft and bright,
> That e'er the midday sun pierc'd through with light;
> Upon his cheeks a lively blush he spread,
> Wash'd from the morning beauties' deepest red;
> An heartless flattering [flaming] meteor shone for hair,
> And fell adown his shoulders with loose care;
> He cuts out a silk mantle from the skies,
> Where the most sprightly azure pleas'd the eyes;
> This he with starry vapours sprinkles [spangles] fall;
> Took in their prime ere they grow ripe and fall;
> Of a new rainbow, ere it fret or fade,
> The choicest piece cut [took] out, a scarfe is made.

"This," Johnson concluded, "is a just specimen of Cowley's imagery: what might in general expressions be great and forcible he weakens and makes ridiculous by branching it into small parts. That Gabriel was invested with the softest or brightest

colours of the sky we might have been told, and been dismissed
to improve the idea in our different proportions of conception;
but Cowley could not let us go till he had related where Gabriel
got first his skin, and then his mantle, then his lace, and then
his scarfe, and related it in the terms of the mercer and the
taylor."[9]

Generally, Cowley's penchant for letting his muse carry him
away was responsible for much of the "fragmentation" in the
Davideis; and Johnson notices this characteristic in his final
remarks: "In the perusal of the *Davideis,* as of all Cowley's
works, we find wit and learning unprofitably squandered. At-
tention has no relief, and the affections are never moved; we are
sometimes surprised, but never delighted, and find much to
admire, but little to approve. Still, however, it is the work of
Cowley, of a mind capacious by nature, and replenished by
study."[10] Cowley never succeeds in presenting an artistic unity
in the poem; it remains a series of incidents, each interesting
for different reasons, all without the thematic and rhetorical
unity of *Paradise Lost.*

As for when the *Davideis* was written, Sprat thought the poem
was a very early one, "wholly written in so young an Age. . . . I
have often heard you [Martin Clifford, Master of Charterhouse]
declare that he had finish'd the greatest part of it while he was
yet a young Student at *Cambridge.*"[11] If Clifford is correct, the
heroic poem was begun as early as 1638 and its four books
substantially completed during the years immediately following.
However, it is unlikely that the poem is a university product.
Nethercot's theory places the poem in the period between 1638
and 1654; there was, he thought, clear evidence of revision trace-
able to periods in Cowley's life. He points to the neo-Platonic
references in Book II ("What are thou, Love"), which indicate
a time about 1641 when Cowley was impressed with the Cam-
bridge Platonists.[12]

But the famous Mrs. Katherine Phillips (the "matchless Or-
inda") referred to a different section of Book II as a "new
thing" in a letter to William Temple of June 15, 1654: "Heer
are some Verses of Cowly's, tell mee how you like them. tis only
a peece taken out of a new thing of his, the whole is very longe
& is a discription of, or rather a paraphrase upon the friendships
of David and Jonathan, tis I think ye best I have seen of his, and
I like ye subject because tis that I would bee perfect In."[13]

Obviously, Cowley had given Mrs. Phillips a revised or new section of Book II, knowing that she and her circle would be interested in the matter of platonic friendship.[14]

However, parts of Book III—the passage on Moab's tapestries—point back to 1641 and to Cowley's possible association with Van Dyck, while Nethercot suggests that the political subject of Book IV refers to the English situation from 1652 to 1653.[15] In 1949, Frank Kermode, who questioned Nethercot's claim for the expanded period of composition, maintained that the poem was wholly the product of the five years from 1650 to 1654, the same years that saw Cowley on the island of Jersey and in France working on the Pindarics. There seemed, he thought, no reason to parallel the poet's topical interests with incidents in the poem.

Kermode's detailed argument is a convincing one; the poem was probably begun in 1651 or 1652 and completed by 1654. Sprat's implication (published in 1668) that the poem was an early one may have been his way of protecting Cowley's reputation in case the Royalists began to consider Book IV an allegory of Puritan or republican apologetics: "If, at the time of the publication of the *Davideis,* Cowley had deserted the royal cause —and this cannot be denied—and if the poem contains, in that book which Nethercot plausibly regards as an allegory—evidence that Cowley was thinking along republican lines, have we not found that Sprat had good reason for pretending that the poem was written (*wholly* written) years before the Common-wealth?[16] Cowley's poem follows Davenant's *Gondibert* and may have been begun under Davenant's encouragement, for certain episodes (Cowley's college of prophets in Judea and Astragon's house in *Gondibert*) are quite similar, and some of the notes reveal the influence of both Davenant and Hobbes. Since Cowley was, however, a member of their circle when Davenant published his poem in 1650, one cannot be sure to what extent *his* ideas are incorporated in Davenant's preface.

In the Preface for the *Poems* of 1656, the *Davideis* receives the most detailed and lengthy discussion. Cowley planned his heroic poem in twelve books:

not for the *Tribes* sake, but after the *Pattern* of our Master *Virgil;* and intended to close all with that most Poetical and excellent *Elegie* of *Davids* on the death of *Saul* and *Jonathan*: For I had no mind to carry him quite on to his *Anointing* at *Hebron,* because it is the custom of *Heroick Poets* (as we see by the examples of *Homer* and

Virgil, whom we should do ill to forsake to imitate others) never to come to the full end of their *Story*; but onely so near, that everyone may see it; as men commonly play not out the game, when it is evident that they can win it, but lay down their Cards, and take up what they have won.[17]

In spite of this grand plan, only four books were completed when, for some reason, Cowley found he "had neither *Leisure* hitherto, nor have *Appetite* at present to finish the work, or so much as to revise that part which is done with that care which I resolved to bestow upon it, and which the *Dignity* of the *Matter* well deserves."[18] Continuing his prefatory argument, he justifies David as hero; for the young shepherd was the ideal man and "greatest *Monarch* . . . the best and mightiest of that Royal Race from whence *Christ* himself, according to the flesh disdained not to descend." An equally important reason for choosing David was that tradition considered him best of poets and a kind of Hebraic Orpheus. Davenant reflected that attitude by naming him greatest of heroic poets: "*Moses, David,* and *Solomon,* for their Songs, Psalmes, and Anthemes,—the Second being the acknowledg'd Favorite of God, whom he had gain'd by excellent Praises in sacred Poesy."[19] Cowley was following the example of his friend Richard Crashaw in turning poetry to "things Divine." The Vergilian epigraph

> *Me verò primùm dulces ante omnia Musae,*
> *Quarum sacra fero ingenti percussus amore,*
> *Accipiant, Coeliq; vias et Sidera monstrent*

(Me indeed first and before all things let the Muses, whose priest I am and whose great love has conquered me, take me up and show me the roadways of the sky and the stars.)[20]

reveals him the priest and devotee of poetry, that "*Divine Science,*" pleading to be shown the mysteries of the pathways in the sky.

The Preface, which concludes as a manifesto about the sacred poem, attacks "senseless *Fables* and *Metamorphoses*" as a waste of wit and eloquence. Writing such falsehoods is merely serving up "the *Cold-meats* of the *Antients,* new-heated, and new set forth";[21] the greatest poetry has truth restored to its original place in poetry, "the clearest light by which they finde the soul who seek it."[22] Diverted from the proper function of poetry,

poets will again find the way in the *Davideis,* a dedicated effort
to make poetry from divine subjects: "What can we imagine
more proper for the ornaments of *Wit* or *Learning* in the story
of *Deucalion,* then in that of *Noah*? why will not the actions of
Sampson afford as plentiful matters as the *Labors* of *Hercules*?
why is not *Jeptha's Daughter* as good *a woman* as *Iphigenia*?
And the friendship of *David* and *Jonathan* more worthy celebra-
tion, then that of *Theseus* and *Perithous*?[23]

But, Cowley warns, poets of the second rank ought not regard
the choice of an Old Testament subject as a guarantee of fame;
for the writing of all poems requires "the same fertility of *In-
vention,* the same wisdom of *Disposition*; the same *Judgment* in
observance of *Decencies*; the same lustre and vigor of *Elocution*;
the same modesty and majestie of *Number.*"[24] "To charm the
people with harmonious precepts" (the phrase is Davenant's),
sacred poesy must seek truths and carefully observe the figures
and metaphors which embody and enliven the truths themselves.
Matters of craft and decorum would be especially important
because of the sanctity of the subject and the priestlike role
of the poet.

That the practical concerns of epic decorum occupied Cowley
is apparent in the great body of notes appended to the epic;
indeed, the practice of Vergil is usually the ultimate sanction
for epic convention in the *Davideis.* An example from Book I
shows him subtly aware of how short lines *look* in his poem
and in Vergil's:

Though none of the *English Poets,* nor indeed of the ancient *Latin,*
have imitated *Virgil* in leaving sometimes half-verses (where the
sense seems to invite a man to that liberty) yet his authority alone
is sufficient, especially in a thing that looks so naturally and gracefully:
and I am far from their opinion, who think that Virgil himself intended
to have filled up those broken *Hemestiques*: There are some places
in him, which I dare almost swear have been made up since his death
by the putid officiousness of some *Grammarians*; as that of Dido,
       ———*Moriamur inultae?*
       Sed moriamur, ait. ———
Here I am confident *Virgil* broke off; and indeed what could be
more proper for the passion she was then in, then to conclude
abruptly with that resolution? Nothing could there be well added.[25]

There are cases where psychological realism demanded an ap-
propriately imperfect line (Cowley's example is Lucifer's painful

cry, "Did I lose *Heav'en* for this?"), and the note anticipates
likely criticism from those wits who believed in the inviolability
of the regular pentameter. Cowley was also capable of breaking
the rules (not by negligence but by intention) to include a line
longer than the normal pentameter, and he cites his precedent:

I am sorry that it is necessary to admonish the most part of *Readers*,
that it is not by negligence that this verse ["Nor can the glory contain
it self in th' endless space"] is so loose, long, and as it were, *Vast*;
it is to paint in the number the nature of the thing which it describes,
which I would have observed in divers other places of this *Poem*, that
else will pass for very careless verses: as before, *And over-runs the
neighb'ring fields with violent course.* In the second Book, *Down a
precipice deep, down he casts them all*—and, *And fell adown his
shoulders with loose care.* In the 3. *Brass was his Helmet, his Boots
Brass, and ore his breast a thick Plate of strong Brass he wore.* In the 4.
Like some fair Pine ore-looking all th'ignobler Wood; and, *Some from
the Rocks cast themselves down headlong;* and many more; but it
is enough to instance in a few. The thing is, that the disposition
of words and numbers should be such, as that out of the order and
sound of them, the things themselves may be represented. This the
Greeks were not so accurate as to bind themselves to; neither have
our *English Poets* observed it, for ought I can find. The *Latins* (*qui
Musas colunt severiores*) sometimes did it, and their *Prince, Virgil,*
always. In whom the examples are innumerable, and taken notice
of by all judicious men, so that it is superfluous to collect them.[26]

Less significant matters also concern Cowley. He considers
even the minor subject of what is natural, pleasing, and poetic
in numbers;[27] he offers caution in the proper placing of adjec-
tives;[28] he advises epic poets to be more restrained in the use
of catalogs than was the practice in Homer (and less spare than
the other extreme in Lucan); and he even worries over the epic
decorum of specific words. "Spouse," he tells us in a note to
Book II, "is not an *Heroical word,*"[29] and the name "Nob" is
"too unheroical."[30] The notes are a wealth of information which
Cowley has gathered to defend virtually every epic practice
(and irregularity) he observes in the poem.

What ultimately concerns Cowley in so many of the notes
is the difference between the truth of event and that of poetry.
How much latitude is permissible when one is working with a
scriptural subject? Cowley obviously accepted the opinion Dave-
nant stated in his preface to *Gondibert*:

But to make great Actions credible is the principall Art of Poets, who, though they avouch the utility of Fictions, should not, by altering and subliming Story, make use of their priviledg [sic] to the detriment of the Reader, whose incredulity, when things are not represented in proportion, doth much allay the rellish of his pity, hope, joy, and other Passions: For we may descend to compare the deceptions in Poesie to those of them that professe dexterity of Hand which resembles Conjuring, and to such we come not with the intention of *Lawyers* to examine the evidence of Facts, but are content, if we like the carriage of their feign'd motion, to pay for being well deceiv'd.[31]

Fictions, then, are useful when they do not exceed the probable; not the heart of the matter, they are simply a device whereby the poet enhances the truth of the event involved. Hobbes's answer to Davenant echoes the same opinion:

For as truth is the bound of Historical, so the Resemblance of truth is the utmost limit of Poeticall Liberty. In old time amongst the Heathen such strange fictions and Metamorphoses were not so remote from the Articles of their Faith as they are now from ours, and therefore were not so unpleasant. Beyond the actual works of nature a Poet may now go; but beyond the conceived possibility of nature, never. I can allow a Geographer to make in the Sea a Fish or a Ship which by the scale of his Mapp would be two or three hundred mile long, and think it done for ornament, because it is done without the precincts of his undertaking; but when he paints an *Elephant* so, I presently apprehend it as ignorance, and a plain confession of *Terra incognita.*[32]

The poet as priest speaks poetic truth, and his poetic logic must not violate the boundaries of the appearance of probability. Deviations from history are excused when a "stroke of Poetry" is more fortuitous than the historical fact; to make dead truth into truth operative necessitates changes to coincide with the logic of fiction. Throughout these notes, Cowley never loses sight of the fact that he is consciously *creating a poem,* not simply versifying scriptural texts; the notes are, therefore, a valuable record of the problems involved when "mortal wit" transforms "heavenly truths" into poetry.

II   *"Polisht Pillars of strong Verse"*

The *Davideis* opens, *in medias res,* with the confrontation of David and Saul sometime after David's victory over Goliath.

Following the proposition and invocation directed to Christ,
Cowley pleads for the "blest rage" to aid him, for his steps
pursue "untrodden paths to *Sacred Fame*";

> Lo, with *pure hands* thy heav'enly *Fires* to take,
> My well-chang'd *Muse* I a chast *Vestal* make!
> From earths vain joys, and loves soft witchcraft free,
> I consecrate my *Magdalena* to Thee!
> Lo, this great work, a Temple to thy praise,
> On polisht *Pillars* of strong *Verse* I raise!
> A *Temple,* where if *Thou* vouchsafe to dwell,
> It *Solomons,* and *Herods* shall excel.
> Too long the *Muses-Land* have *Heathen* bin;
> Their *Gods* too long were *Dev'ils,* and *Vertues Sin*;
> But *Thou, Eternal Word,* hast call'd forth *Me*
> Th' *Apostle,* to convert that *World* to *Thee,*
> T' unbind the charms that in slight *Fables* lie,
> And teach that *Truth* is *truest Poesie*.[33]

His muse, a "chast *Vestal*" who tends the "heav'enly [sic] *Fires*,"
is transformed into his Magdalene, free from the vanity of the
Pindarics and the sensuality of *The Mistress*. Like Herbert's,
Cowley's poem becomes a temple raised on the pillars of verse
as the words of epic poetry are rededicated to Christ, Himself
the eternal word.

From a Saul ready to come to a new agreement with David,
against whom his hate but little prevails, the focus shifts to hell
for Cowley's version of the underworld. Hades and its Beelzebub
are both insufficient to frighten or convince: one is only a place
of solid darkness; the other, a pasteboard demon going through
the contortions of disappointment, knocking his iron teeth,
howling, frowning, and darting red flames from his eyes. Among
the minor devils, the figure of Envy, who answers her master's
plea for volunteers to subvert Saul's good intentions, is from a
typical Gothic melodrama; Milton may have remembered her
as he sketched his terrible figures of Sin and Death:

> *Envy* at last crawls forth from that dire throng,
> Of all the direful'st; her black locks hung long,
> Attir'd with curling *Serpents;* her pale skin
> Was almost dropt from the sharp bones within,
> And at her breast stuck *Vipers* which did prey
> Upon her panting heart, both night and day
> Sucking black *bloud* from thence, which to repair

> Both night and day they left fresh *poysons* there.
> Her garments were deep stain'd in humane gore,
> And torn by her own hands, in which she bore
> A knotted whip, and bowl, that to the brim
> Did with green gall, and juice of wormwood swim.
> With which when she was drunk, she furious grew
> And lasht *herself*; thus from th' accursed crew,
> *Envy*, the worst of *Fiends*, herself presents,
> *Envy, good* only when she herself *torments*.[34]

In her classic exemplum of Cain and Abel, Envy herself reveals how little individual life she has. "I saw him fling the *stone*," she says, "as if he meant, / At once his *Murder* and his *Monument*." Suddenly Envy is too clever, too contrived; and the immediacy and bitterness which she ought to convey is lost in the witty lines Cowley assigns her. He has failed in presenting the illusion of truth in his portrait of hell and its inhabitants.

A complementary scene in heaven dramatically balances the hellish activities, but the contrasts are not subtly accomplished. The reader is always aware of the mechanically drawn parallels between the two locales, for each is the converse of the other. The repetition of the words "beneath" and "above" stresses direction, but directions are completely without the complex moral associations they have in Milton's epic.[35] Each description opens with lines parallel to the other:

> There is a place deep, wondrous deep below.[36]
> [and]
> There is a place o'reflown with hallowed Light.[37]

The parallels continue throughout the descriptions:

> Beneath the dens where *unfletcht Tempests lye.*
> . . . .
>
> Beneath the mighty *Oceans* wealthy Caves.
>
> Beneath th'eternal *Fountain* of all Waves.[38]
>
> Above the subtle foldings of the Sky.
> Above the well-set *Orbs* soft *Harmony.*
> Above those petty *Lamps* that guild the *Night*.[39]

Each domain has its own ruler: one is capable only of disorder and destruction; the other, all order and all creation. The great

forces, their leaders, and the major locales in the combat have
been sketched early. Although the battles take place on earth
between men, each man has his particular sanction which indi-
cates his moral position in the struggle.

The poem's first digression on the power of music closely
follows the preparatory exposition. When David is asked to play
and sing to cure Saul's "fantastick rage," the poet himself asks
the muse to tell him of the power that dwells in the "blest
Numbers":

> Tell me, oh *Muse* (for *Thou*, or none canst tell
> The mystick pow'ers that in blest *Numbers* dwell,
> Thou their great *Nature* know'st, nor is it fit
> This noblest *Gem* of thine own *Crown* t'omit)
> Tell me from whence these heav'enly charms arise;
> Teach the dull world t'admire what they *despise*.[40]

Just as the poet composes his music "till all the parts and words
their places take," so was the world, "*Gods Poem*," created.
Cowley has, he explains, St. Augustine and Scripture for his
sources "that the World was made in *Number, Weight,* and
Measure; which are all qualities of a good *Poem*. This order and
proportion of things is the true *Musick* of the world, and not that
which *Pythagoras, Plato, Tully, Macrob,* and many of the *Fathers*
imagined, to arise audibly from the circumvolution of the
Heavens. This is their *musical* and loud voice, of which *David*
speaks, *Psalm* 19."[41] God was the primary poet, the creation the
archetypal song:

> *Water,* and *Air* he for the *Tenor* chose,
> *Earth* made the *Base,* the *Treble Flame* arose,
> To th' active *Moon* a quick brisk stroke he gave,
> To *Saturns string* a touch more soft and grave.
> The *motions Strait,* and *Round,* and *Swift,* and *Slow,*
> And *Short,* and *Long,* were mixt and woven so,
> Did in such artful *Figures* smoothly fall,
> As made this decent measur'd *Dance* of *All.*
> And this is *Musick; Sounds* that charm our ears,
> Are but one *Dressing* that rich *Science* wears.
> Thou no man hear't, though no man it reherse,
> Yet will there still be *Musick* in my *Verse*.[42]

Man, as part of this great dance, is a naturally harmonious
creature, a "*single Quire*" allied to the greater song by the

sympathy he has with the maker. So it is that music heals human wounds (here metaphors of disharmony) by tuning the disorder into harmony. The body hears one note and longs naturally to be in tune with it: "Thus when two *Brethren strings* are set alike, / To *move* them *both,* but *one* of them we *strike.*"[43]

The digression serves a double purpose: it emphasizes the power of the sacred poetry which one is now reading, and it introduces David as Hebraic Orpheus, the musician of cosmic harmony whose songs are analogous to those of the Divine. The section concludes with David's song itself, Psalm 114, "When *Israel* was from bondage led"; but, during the theme sung by the "wise *Charmers* healthful voice," Saul feigns drowsiness and sleep in order not to strike out at David again. The episode has convinced one of Saul's malignancy.

Fleeing from Saul's rage, David first returns to his home, "a small, but artful *Paradise,*" and to his wife Michol; then he moves on to Samuel's College of Prophets, a proportioned, orderly, and delightful court composed of doctors, companions, and scholars whose lives are passed in a kind of academic Shangri-La:

> The *House* was a large *Square;* but plain and low;
> Wise *Natures* use *Art* strove not to outgo.
> An inward Square by well-rang'd *Trees* was made;
> And midst the friendly cover of their shade,
> A pure, well-tasted, wholsome *Fountain* rose;
> Which no vain cost of *Marble* did enclose;
> Nor through carv'd *shapes* did the for'ced waters pass,
> *Shapes* gazing on themselves i'th' *liquid glass.*
> Yet the chaste stream that 'mong loose peebles fell
> For *Cleanness, Thirst, Religion* serv'd as well.[44]

The idea of a philosophical college had always interested Cowley, and such descriptions were conventional in utopian literature. Here the great ones engaged in various tasks: Nathan studied the orderly heavens; Seriah, history; Samuel, God's law. All were occupied in discovering the prevailing cosmic order and then in reflecting this order in their work. Since the proper end of knowledge for them was to know God better, their poets, Heman and Asaph, sang the creation and celebrated the Law, praising God's poem by relating the Creation of the universe from an "unshap'd kind of *Something.*" To this ideal college

Saul twice sent troops to apprehend David, and twice the men
were won over to the peaceful pursuits of the prophets:

> They came, but a new spirit their hearts possest,
> Scatt'ring a sacred calm through every brest:
> The furrows of their brow, so rough erewhile,
> Sink down into the dimples of a *Smile*.
> Their cooler veins swell with a peaceful tide,
> And the chaste streams with even current glide.
> A sudden *day* breaks gently through their eyes,
> And *Morning-blushes* in their cheeks arise.
> The thoughts of war, of blood, and murther cease;
> In peaceful tunes they adore the *God* of *Peace*.[45]

God's harmonies do act upon men who have not deliberately
chosen evil above good.

Book I is organized around the concept of order and harmony
in the universe. Forces of chaos and disorder in Saul have their
champions in Beelzebub and Envy; their adversary is the divine
poet David, in whose poems the word is ritualistically embodied.
Some men, unconvinced of God's word in nature, may be won
over by its surrogate in art. Others, like Saul, who refuse to
recognize the analogy and whose hearts are blackened, will be
blinded to the truth of heavenly music and lost forever.

Cowley's interests in Book II are primarily historical. Much
of the book is concerned with a pageant of Abraham's career and
with David's vision of "*a* Prophesie *of all the succession of his
Race till* Christs *time*." Rather than continue the narrative directly,
Cowley elaborates the subject by extending the limits of the
poem back in time and then into the future to parallel the geo-
graphic extension from Hell to Heaven of the initial book; such
contrast is a favorite technique in the *Davideis*. Book II opens
with a description of the friendship between David and Jonathan
and a "*digression concerning the nature of* Love." Saul's enmity
has its counterpart in his son's friendship with David.

Cowley discusses the famous friendship in terms of con-
temporary neo-Platonic attitudes which interested Katherine
Phillips and her circle. Love, the great mystery, is the primary
power which maintains order in the world; but, as Cowley indi-
cates in a series of questions, men are completely ignorant of
how it operates. Even in the non-human world, its strength is
felt as it weds iron to loadstone and ivy to oak, but its "chief

Palace is *Mans Heart* alone." Cowley extends his metaphor to make a religion of love:

> Thousand with *Joys* cluster around thine head,
> O're which a gall-less *Dove* her wings does spread,
> A gentle *Lamb,* purer and whiter farre
> Then *Consciences* of thine own *Martyrs* are,
> Lies at thy feet; and thy right hand does hold
> The mystick *Scepter* of a *Cross* of Gold.[46]

The holy union between two "doves" offered occasion for all sorts of wonderful paradoxes to explain the relationship:

> They both were *Servants,* they both *Princes* were.
> If any Joy to one of them was sent,
> It was most his, to whom it least was meant,
> And fortunes malice betwixt both was crost,
> For striking one, it wounded th'other most.[47]

Purified of all earthly dross and material (thus surpassing wedded love), the love of David and Jonathan is so perfect that no additional refinements are possible. Like angels on earth, the two young men share in the power which guarantees the cosmic order.

Friendship leads Jonathan to search out the depth of his father's "wound," and his presence at Saul's great feast gives Cowley the opportunity to include the pageant of sacrifice and a description of Saul's ten Syrian tapestries. "The custom," Cowley writes, "of having Stories wrought in *Hangings, Coverlits,* nay even wearing *Garments,* is made to be very ancient by the poets."[48] None of the events of Abraham's story, however, draws as much attention as the scene where the patriarch, secure in God's love, prepares to sacrifice Isaac. This scene is an ironic commentary on the ensuing incident in which Saul denounces his son, "sacrificing" him to his own jealousies. The differences between the two fathers are underscored by the proximity of the episodes; Saul's actions are unlike those of his ancestors and even more unlike those of Christ; for the spirit of love, with which the book began, is foreign to him.

David's great vision, stimulated by *"Phansie"* and her coach of "shapes and airy *Forms,"* and organized by an angel who

> . . . finds them mingled in an antique dance;
> Of all the numerous forms fit choice he takes,
> And joyns them wisely, and this *Vision* makes,[49]

celebrates the great victories of the future king, passes on to
the wit of Solomon and his pomp and wealth; to Solomon's son,
and Abijah, Asan, Josaphat; and to many, many more examples
from Kings and Chronicles. War, conquest, destruction, sin, and
death characterize human history until the birth of Christ. At
that event, heralded by the appearance of Joseph, war gives way
to the realm of angels and "blew-ey'd *violets*," to lilies and roses
in a garden-like Eden. A human maid hears the heavenly
message: "Hail thou, who must *Gods wife, Gods mother* be!"
Amazed at the paradox, David is assured of the vision's truth
by Gabriel, disguised as a "comely *youth*": "From thy blest seed
shall spring / The promis'd *Shilo*, the great *Mystick King*."[50]

The central part of Book III is devoted to the interpolated
narrative of David and Goliath. This book presents David in
exile, first in Nobe, then in Gath (where he feigns madness to
avoid assassination), and finally in the land of another exile,
Ruth of Moab. And, at Moab's court, the reader is ready for "the
descriptions of worthy circumstances [which] are necessary ac-
cessions to a Poem, and being well performed are the Jewels
and the most precious ornaments of Poesy."[51] The pageant of
honorable royalty is presided over by the bard, Melchor, whose
subjects are, appropriately, "*Nature's* secrets," and whose songs
are "the sawce of *Moabs* noble feast":

> He sung what *Spirit*, through the whole *Mass* is *spread*,
> Ev'ry where *All*; how *Heavens Gods Law* approve,
> And think it *Rest* eternally to *Move*.
> How the kind *Sun* usefully comes and goes,
> Wants it himself, yet gives to Man repose.[52]

When Melchor concludes, Joab, at popular request, narrates
the episode of David and Goliath. Even as a child, Joab begins,
David's Orphean songs were like Melchor's:

> Scarce past a *Child*, all wonders would he sing
> Of *Natures Law*, and *Pow'er* of *Natures King*.
> His *sheep* would scorn their food to hear his lay,
> And savage *Beasts* stand by as *tame* as they.
> The fighting *Winds* would stop there, and admire;
> Learning *Consent* and *Concord* from his Lyre.
> *Rivers*, whose waves roll'd down aloud before;
> Mute, as their *Fish*, would listen to'wards the *shore*.[53]

The narrative is a familiar one, and Cowley's version adds little of special note. David's sense of mission, Saul's entreaty, the double challenge, Goliath's defeat, Jonathan's admiration—all are rapidly sketched in less than a hundred and fifty couplets. Cowley does handle well the ensuing courtship of David and Michol, and the same space is given to this episode as to the encounter with the Philistine champion. Obviously, the domestic David is of equal interest to Cowley, and the delineation of Saul's daughters, Merab and Michol, is skillfully done.

Of the two girls, the younger Michol, withdrawn and shy, is softer and gentler; men rejoice to obey her. Merab, on the other hand, is cool, distant, haughty, but no less beautiful. The two are copies—one of Saul; the other of Jonathan. The elder conveniently disdain the lowborn, country boy David for Adriel, more "suitable" to her position, while David and Michol fall in love at first sight. Which loved first it is impossible to say:

> Ev'en so (methinks) when two Fair *Tapers* come,
> From several Doors entring at once the Room,
> With a swift flight that leaves the Eye behind;
> Their *amorous Lights* into *one Light* are join'd.
> *Nature* herself, were she to judge the case,
> Knew not which first *began* the kind embrace.[54]

Even Michol could not resist the *"Tyrant Custom,"* but her coquetry and "cold *Indifferency"*—"the *formal decencies* of virgin-shame"—are overcome by David's song and Jonathan's pleas. The courtship song is one of the fine lyric moments of the *Davideis*:

> Awake, awake my *Lyre,*
> And tell thy *silent Masters* humble tale,
> In sounds that may prevail;
> Sounds that gentle thoughts inspire,
> Though so *Exalted* she
> And I so *Lowly* be,
> Tell her such *diffe'rent Notes* make all thy *Harmonie.*

> Hark, how the Strings awake,
> And though the *Moving Hand* approach not near,
> A kind of num'erous *Trembling* make.
> Now all thy Forces try,
> Now all thy charms apply,
> Revenge upon her *Ear* the *Conquests* of her *Eye.*

Weak *Lyre!* thy vertue sure
Is useless here, since thou art only found
To *Cure,* but not to *Wound,*
And she to *Wound,* but not to *Cure,*
Too weak too wilt thou prove
My *Passion* to remove,
Physick to other *Ills,* thou'rt *Nourishment* to *Love.*

Sleep, sleep again, my Lyre,
For thou can'st never tell my humble tale
In sounds that will prevail.
Nor gentle thoughts in her inspire;
All they vain mirth lay by,
Bid thy strings silent ly,
Sleep, sleep again, my *Lyre,* and let thy *Master dy.*[55]

Saul's envy is thwarted with David's pledge of a "double *Dowre,*
two hundred foreskins brought / Or choice *Philistian* Knights";
and the book concludes with a magnificent pageant, the "moving
Galaxy" of David's wedding.

Throughout books II and III, Cowley's epic has been a quite
conventional fusion of sacred material into a congenial Classical
pattern; but Book IV—Saul's rise to power and Jonathan's heroic
deeds at Nahas—presents a new problem. Cowley may have
intended the first part of the fourth book to mirror aspects of
the contemporary political scene from 1652 to the establishment
of the Protectorate on December 15, 1653; but, if so, there is
no consistent allegorical scheme. The vague correspondences are
not clear, and the fact that David's career was a favorite allegor-
ical theme for both Royalist and Roundhead makes allegorical
interpretation difficult. Although one could expect an allegory
published by him in 1656 to be pro-Cromwellian, it is unlikely
that Cowley would have equated Cromwell with Saul; for, if
Cowley had, David, the hero in exile and the true leader of
Israel, would have had to be Charles. Besides, in Cowley's narra-
tive, Saul wanted to be king and was fated to be so; Cromwell
always disclaimed any personal ambition for kingship. There
is no question, however, that, to his enemies, Cromwell would
be analogous to Saul and that, following the Restoration, Cowley
could stand to gain by such a reading.

In the years of composition before Cowley returned to Eng-
land, however, he may have had some such resemblance between

Cromwell and Saul in mind (Samuel and his weak sons could easily represent the Long Parliament and its successor, the Barebones Parliament). One can only guess, however, lacking manuscript copies of the poem and its revisions and early versions, that such may once have been the proposed intent of Book IV. Finding himself in a political position hardly favorable to the Protectorate, and having been recently imprisoned as a Royalist spy, Cowley may have changed Book IV so that it is impossible to reconstruct from it a clear scheme.

Not wishing to go on record against kingship, for there were those who wished to re-establish the monarchy with relatives of Charles or with Cromwell himself, Cowley extended the debate over kingship and suspended his narrative. Samuel had complained that kingship was always synonymous with tyranny and oppression, but here Moab interrupts with a defense of constitutional monarchy:

> The good old *Seer* 'gainst *Kings* was too severe.
> 'Tis *Jest* to tell a *People* that they're *Free,*
> *Who,* or *How many* shall their *Masters* be
> Is the sole doubt; *Laws guid,* but cannot *reign;*
> And though they *bind* not Kings, yet they *restrain.*
> I dare affirm (so much I trust their *Love*)
> That no one *Moabite* would his speech approve.[56]

In reply, Samuel admonishes:

> Tis true, Sir, he replies;
> Yet men whom age and action renders wise,
> So much great changes fear, that they believe,
> All evils *will,* which *may* from them arise.[57]

As a footnote to the entire discussion, Cowley adds two comments to let his reader understand he is not against kingship, and that Samuel is not accurate in equating monarchy with tyranny: "The *Israelites* knew they were to be governed at last by *kings* [as many Englishmen did in 1653]. . . . They desired it by reason of the great disorders and afflictions which they suffered for want of it." And Cowley comments later, "It is a vile opinion of those men, and might be punished without *Tyranny,* if they teach it, who hold, that the *right* of *Kings* is set down by *Samuel* in this place. Neither did the people of Israel ever allow, or the *Kings* avow the assumption of such a power, as appears by the story of Ahab and Naboth. Some indeed did exercise it, but that is no more a proof of the *Right,* then their *Practise* was of the *Lawfulness* of *Idolatry."*[58]

In these extremely topical arguments, which may belong to the year that saw the crown offered to Cromwell and his establishment as Protector, Cowley emphasizes that there is no special biblical injunction against monarchy; and he carefully separates his personal opinion about kings (and his interpretation of the biblical comments on monarchy) from that of his character Samuel.

The remainder of this final book of the epic (following the description of Saul's coronation) is devoted to the deeds of Jonathan and his perfect servant, Abdon, in the battle against the Philistines at Gilgal. Alone the two men scout the enemy stronghold, each killing his counterpart—an enemy hero, Elcanor, and his retainer—and then, inspired by God, they rage into the enemy camp to kill thousands. Jonathan pauses from the killing only long enough to eat some honey found in a nearby tree. Saul, in another part of the field and unaware of his son's great victory, had rashly doomed his own son when he ordered any man killed who would that day take time from the battle to eat or drink. Cowley's biblical sources provide an excellent conclusion: Jonathan is saved by the people who rebel against the edict of King Saul, and the incident illustrates how monarchs are restrained from acting as Samuel had predicted they would: they cannot always be permitted to let *"guidless Passion"* lead their will. At this point Cowley's epic breaks off, Moab and David reach "th'appointed place; / Well-chosen and well-furnisht for the chase" and for additional interpolated narratives. But the poem remains unfinished.

This summary cannot conceal the great weakness of the *Davideis*—its mechanical nature. As a scholar, Cowley knew all the epic conventions and could argue and document every line of the poem with correspondences from his epic predecessors. The parts always remain as such, for he had neither the facility nor the strength to give the conventions life in his own poem. One remembers the *Davideis* as an epic "collage"—a collection of separately interesting incidents and digressions which are never synthesized. Cowley must have seen that his gift in the epic was analytic; he did not possess the magic to bring to harmony the diverse strains of epic materials.

CHAPTER 6

"*A* small House *and a* large Garden"

I "I *hear* Fames Trumpet"

THE Restoration did not bring Cowley the recognition he deserved. His public profession of loyalty—the magnificent nineteen-stanza ode "*Upon His Majesties* Restoration and Return" —published on May 31, 1660 (two days following Restoration day)—won him little immediate favor from the monarch he served so well in France. Cowley's trips back and forth across the channel had made him suspect to both Royalists and Parliamentarians, and a section omitted by the cautious Sprat in 1668 from the Preface of 1656 had not won him friends in the king's party.

In the omitted section Cowley had rationally and judiciously advised men to forget their previous enmity—to give up "Names of Party, and *Titles* of *Division*"—and had suggested that no writer perpetuate previous struggles but practice instead the "*Art* of *Oblivion.*" Cowley's plea for continued peace and self-discipline contained his confession that he had burned works of his own which might have initiated new quarrels or intensified older ones. He had, he admitted, dealt with himself more severely than any officer of the state could have.[1] Later, after the Restoration, Sprat found himself embarrassed by Cowley's political repudiation of Royalist sympathies, and he did what he could to excuse the poet's statements. Sprat, who insisted that Cowley was simply advising Charles's supporters to remain quiet as a matter of temporary expediency, succeeded in twisting Cowley's honest statement into a Machiavellian position:

In this case perhaps it were not enough to alledge for him to men of moderate minds, that what he there said was published before a book of Poetry, and so ought rather to be esteemed as a Probleme of his Fancy and Invention than as the real Image of his Judgment. . . . He therefore believed that it would be a meritorious service to the King, if any man who was known to have followed

his interest could insinuate into the Usurpers minds, that men of
his Principles were now willing to be quiet, and could perswade the
poor oppressed Royalists to conceal their affections for better
occasions.[2]

Solicitations on behalf of Cowley by Lord Albans (Jermyn) and
the Marquis of Ormonde did not succeed in pacifying Charles,[3]
who, according to William Davenant, had refused to allow
Cowley to kiss his hand.[4] Charles did, however, see that the
fellowship at Trinity was returned; but the poet's great dis-
appointment was in losing the income from the Mastership of
the Savoy, a post given instead to Dr. Gilbert Seldon. Anthony
à Wood claimed Cowley had been deprived "by certain enemies
of the Muses,"[5] but there is no proof. Cowley's sole reward from
the crown was some land in Kent given him in 1662 by Queen
Henrietta Maria for services rendered her during exile.[6]

"*To the* Royal Society," which indicates Cowley's continued
interest in Baconian attitudes and the New Philosophy, is the
other great ode from this period.[7] Cowley was a spokesman for
the "college," and Sprat considered his prose essay, *A Proposition
for the Advancement of Experimental Philosophy,* a crucial docu-
ment in the formation of the society which Cowley had joined
in 1662, its first year.[8] Printed in 1667 as the dedicatory poem
to Sprat's *A History of the Royal Society,* this fine ode laments
the inertia Philosophy had suffered for "three or four thousand
years" because of "Autoritie." Cowley indicted those who had
betrayed Philosophy, those who led it into the paths of vain
and false speculative discourse; Philosophy had been fed with
airy fancies and insubstantial "desserts" and sports, he had been
weakened and his true strength drained by those who sought to
turn him away from true speculation on the empirical data in
"Natures endlesse Treasurie." Cowley's champion, bound to
slavery and therefore to perpetual infancy by the scholastic
establishment, however, found a strong advocate to assume his
cause:

> *Bacon* at last, a mighty Man, arose
>   Whom a wise King and Nature chose
>   Lord Chancellour of both their Lawes
> And boldly undertook the injur'd Pupils cause.[9]

Bacon, the champion of his age against that false god "Autoritie,"
showed man the error of proceeding from words to things; he

insisted upon strict observation of natural phenomena: "The real object must command / Each Judgment of his Eye, and Motion of his Hand." Cowley considered the length of a lifetime insufficient to demonstrate all truths; the stanza lamenting Bacon's mortality is one of the best in the poem, a synthesis of the personal and the formal. To "*Gideon's* little Band" that formed the Royal Society (a group not without its enemies), God had entrusted the task of freeing all "lands" still held in bondage. The group had already demonstrated that

> Natures great Workes no distance can obscure,
> No smalness her near Objects can secure
>> Y' have taught the curious Sight to press
>> Into the privatest recess
> Of her imperceptible Littleness.
>> Y' have learn'd to Read her smallest Hand,
> And well begun her deepest Sense to Understand.[10]

The final stanza concerns Bacon, greatest of philosophers who, like Hobbes, was a "poet" in the most complete sense. Both discovered new lands, and with eyes cleared of old errors, both wrote of those lands with clarity and grace:

> With Courage and Success you the bold work begin;
>> Your Cradle has not Idle bin:
> None e're but *Hercules* and you could be
> At five years Age worthy a History.
>> And ne're did Fortune better yet
>> Th' Historian to the Story fit:
>> As you from all Old Errors free
> And purge the Body of Philosophy;
>> So from all Modern Folies He
> Has vindicated Eloquence and Wit.
> His candid Stile like a clean Stream does slide,
>> And his bright Fancy all the way
> Does like the Sun-shine in it play;
> It does like *Thames,* the best of Rivers, glide,
> Where the God does not rudely overturn,
>> But gently pour the Crystal Urn,
> And with judicious hand does the whole Current Guide.
> T' has all the Beauties Nature can impart,
> And all the comely Dress without the paint of Art.[11]

But Cowley was not totally occupied by his interests in the new philosophy during the early years of the Restoration. His

friend, William Davenport, manager of the "Opera" in Lincoln's
Inn's Fields (and who split shares with Cowley to provide him
a handsome income from the theater),[12] probably encouraged
the revision of the old comedy, *The Guardian*. Cowley, who re-
worked the play, omitted the figure of Dogrel, making Col Cutter
a mere pretender; added several other figures; and properly
satirized Puritans and idealized young love. When the new
version was produced on December 16, 1661, it had a popular
cast; Betterton played Colonel Jolly, the Royalist whose estates
had been confiscated; Mrs. Betterton, the spicy Aurelia; and the
great comedian Nokes, Puny, the would-be intellect.

The play, Downes informs us, "being Acted so perfectly Well
and Exact, it was performed a whole Week with a full Audi-
ence."[13] "A very good play it is," Pepys recorded, for he was
there the first night (the prices were doubled so he sat in the
cheaper gallery seats). Thomas Sprat was in the audience, and
so was the young Dryden; unfortunately, Cowley himself could
not attend because of the death of his brother.[14] Evidently there
was some furor that night, for John Dennis tells us that the play
"was barbarously treated" (Pepys mentions no disturbance at
all), and Downes notes that "the Play was not a little injurious
to the Cavalier Indigent Officers: especially the character of
Cutter and Worm."[15] Others, as Cowley's later preface relates,
attacked the play for its so-called profaneness. That night "Mr.
Cowley received the news of his ill success, not with so much
firmness, as might have been expected from so great a man."[16]

Disappointed with the Savoy and in ill graces with the King
and the more hot-headed Cavaliers, Cowley found himself idol-
ized and successful with everyone except those he tried hardest
to please, the Royalists. Literary accomplishments were not
enough; unlike Horace, he wanted also to be the favorite of
the court. "The Melancholy Cowley," as he called himself, was
playfully upbraided for such vain aspirations by his own Muse;
seeking fame in the world, he had forgotten the ephemeral nature
of popularity. He had, the Muse claimed, acted the role of the
prodigal son, wasting his youth and estate and repenting too late
of his waywardness. Having betrayed his talents and his Muse,
he became "bewitcht with noise and show":

> Wouldst into Courts and Cities from me go;
> Wouldst see the World abroad, and have a share

    In all the follies, and the Tumults there,
    Thou would'st, forsooth, be something in a State,
    And business thou would'st find, and would'st Create!
        Business! the frivolous pretence
    Of humane Lusts to shake off Innocence;
        Business! the grave impertinence;
    Business! the thing which I of all things hate,
    Business! the contradiction of thy Fate.[17]

Cowley had experienced enough of the world of "business"; from then on, he sought retirement in Kent.

II *"This busie World and I shall ne're agree"*

Cowley's final years were spent in the country at Barn Elms from 1663 to 1665, and at Chertsey from 1665 until his death on July 28, 1667. In 1663 he published his *Verses, Lately Written upon Several Occasions,* a small edition consisting of poems which he had not intended to publish until a pirated version published in Dublin forced him to issue his own text. Most of the verses are Pindarics admirably suited to the formal celebrations he had in mind. The volume contained "Christ's Passion" (1656?), a continuation of the religious themes of the *Davideis;* an ode on the occasion of receiving a copy of Broghill's verses (1657); a playful poem to commemorate his gift of a copy of the 1656 edition to the Oxford library (1657?); an important ode on the scientist, Dr. Harvey (1657); a personal remembrance of Alexander Lindsay, Earl of Balcarres, who died in 1659; and other occasional pieces.

    The best example of Cowley's method in this collection, however, has the expansive title, "Ode. *Sitting and Drinking in the Chair, made out of the Reliques of Sir* Francis Drake's *Ship."* Drinking and musing in the famous relic, the poet evokes in his opening stanza the excitement of sea adventures; but the reader knows the persons is sailing only on the "sea of Drink":

    Chear up my Mates, the wind does fairly blow,
        Clap on more sail and never spare;
        Farewell all Lands, for now we are
        In the wide Sea of Drink, and merrily we go.
    Bless me, 'tis hot! another bowl of wine,
        And we shall cut the Burning Line:
    Hey Boyes! she scuds away, and by my head I know,

> We round the World are sailing now.
> What dull men are those who tarry at home,
> When abroad they might wantonly rome,
>> And gain such experience, and spy too
>> Such Countries, and Wonders as I do?
> But prythee good *Pilot* take heed what you do,
>> And fail not to touch at *Peru*;
>> With Gold, there the Vessel we'll store,
>> And never, and never be poor,
>> No never be poor any more.[18]

As the poet realizes that his chair, for all its quiet now, really was once round the world, he grows more contemplative, and his vision expands until he sees it as "the only Universal Chair." The chair has no famous myth associated with it, nor is it celebrated as a constellation; and Cowley thinks it appropriate that, since the chair once made journeys of discovery, people now journey to see it. But the greatest conceit is the final one: the reputation of the chair will spread (a kind of traveling); and, with fame as the breeze, the chair will "run" round the world again. So it is possible, by sitting in it, to take a voyage and yet remain in the same place; stanza one has, as it were, "come true." The result is a freshly proven cliché: one circumnavigates with a verse for a sail and a poet for a pilot without ever leaving his chair. Deptford's Horace and England's Pindar have never been more compatible.

In rural Deptford, where one of Cowley's neighbors was John Evelyn, the poet wrote his Latin poems and finished eleven short essays; these last were published posthumously in his collected works as *Several Discourses by way of Essays, in Verse and Prose*. The essays represent Cowley's last writings, for all except *"The Danger of Procrastination"* are from the period 1665 to 1667.[19] Read, as Sprat informs one they are meant to be, "as a real Character of his own thoughts upon the point of his Retirement," the essays were to have been greatly enlarged and the volume dedicated to St. Albans as "a testimony of his entire respects to him, and a kind of Apology for having left humane Affairs, in the strength of his Age, when he might still have been serviceable to his Country."[20]

Cowley celebrates in these essays the Horatian ideal, so unlike his earlier desire for public recognition, as in the lines of "The Motto": "What shall I do to be for ever known, / And make

the *Age to come* my own?" There the *"Muses Hannibal"* vowed
to cut through *"Unpast Alpes"* led on by *"Fames Trumpet"* to
"Honors, or Estate." Now the goal is rural solitude and sabine
contentment—a retirement theme that became a literary attitude
in the eighteenth century. Cowley's political and personal disap-
pointments were intensely felt; and, although he may have
hoped for a haven in the country, he soon realized that Arcadia
existed only in literary romances.[21]

Although these essays in verse and prose belong to the
seventeenth-century essay tradition of Bacon, Jonson, Hall, Peach-
am, Clarendon, and Boyle, their personal informality suggests
a greater affinity with later writers in that genre, especially
Johnson and Goldsmith.[22] Readers who have found little to
praise in Cowley's poems frequently have singled out the plain,
honest voice and clarity of style in these little "chapters"; and
seven separate editions between 1886 and 1923 indicate their
continued popularity. "But still I love the language of his heart,"
commented Pope in his "Epistle to Augustus" (1737); and the
famous Elia—Lamb—thought Cowley's prose "delicious."

Writing to Coleridge, Lamb asked for his "opinion of a poet,
very dear to me, the now out of fashion Cowley—favor me with
your judgment of him, and tell me if his prose essays, in par-
ticular, as well as no inconsiderable part of his verse, be not
delicious. I prefer the graceful rambling of his essays, even to the
courtly elegance and ease of Addison—abstracting from this
the latter's exquisite humour."[23] Johnson praised their natural-
ness and "smooth and placid equability":

After so much criticism on his Poems, the Essays which accompany
them must not be forgotten. What is said by Sprat of his conver-
sation, that no man could draw from it any suspicion of his excellence
in poetry, may be applied to these compositions. No author ever kept
his verse and his prose at a greater distance from each other. His
thoughts are natural, and his style has a smooth and placid equability,
which has never yet obtained its due commendation. Nothing is far-
sought, or hard laboured; but all is easy without feebleness, and
familiar without grossness.[24]

In two obvious ways the essays are unique: each concludes
with poems or verse translations, usually from Horace, Martial,
or Vergil; and the entire group is unified by a single theme:
"Bene qui latuit, bene vixit." Happy is he "who has a moderate

Minde and Fortune, and lives in the conversation of two or
three agreeable friends, with little commerce in the world
besides, who is esteemed well enough by his few neighbours
that know him, and is truly irreproachable by any body, and
so after a healthful quiet life, before the great inconveniences
of old age, goes more silently out of it then he came in, (for I
would not have him so much as Cry in the *Exit*)."[25] The last
essay, *"Of My self,"* with its summary review of the poet's
career and its epitaph for the living Cowley, is an obvious con-
clusion to the earlier material.

Essay four, *"Of Agriculture,"* may have been first in the
order of composition.[26] The subject is an important one for
Cowley; and, for our delight, it concludes with five verse selec-
tions. The essay opens with a consideration of Vergil as best
husbandman and best philosopher. The two employments were
closely associated in Cowley's mind, for both represent with-
drawal from man's into God's world, and both are concerned
with first principles: "Earth, Water, Air, and the Sun." A para-
graph reminiscent of Bacon's aphoristic style contrasts city and
country:

We are here among the vast and noble Scenes of Nature; we are
there among the pitiful shifts of Policy: We walk here in the light
and open wayes of the Divine Bounty; we grope there in the dark
and confused Labyrinths of Human Malice: Our Senses are here
feasted with the clear and genuine taste of their Objects, which are
all Sophisticated there, and for the most part overwhelmed with
their contraries. Here Pleasure looks (methinks) like a beautiful,
constant, and modest Wife; it is there an impudent, fickle, and painted
Harlot. Here is harmless and cheap *Plenty,* there guilty and expense-
ful Luxury.[27]

Even poetry, "born among the Shepherds," enters the discussion
since verse owes its origins to the country.[28] Cowley's contention,
however, that poetry cannot thrive in the city is fantastic. Cer-
tainly great poems have always been produced in urban environ-
ments. But Cowley has in mind poets like David, Hesiod, and
Homer, pastoral songs and pastoral figures like Homer's Eumaeus.
Cowley's first and favorite example is always Vergil and the
Georgics; even in the *Aneid,* that poet

could not abstain in his great and Imperial Poem from describing
Evander, one of his best Princes, as living just after the homely

manner of an ordinary Countreyman. He seats him in a Throne of
Maple, and lays him but upon a Bears skin, the Kine and Oxen are
lowing in his Court yard, the Birds under the Eeves of his Window
call him up in the morning, and when he goes abroad, only two
Dogs go along with him for his guard: at last when he brings *Aeneas*
into his Royal Cottage, he makes him say this memorable complement,
greater than ever yet was spoken at the *Escurial,* the *Louvre,* or
our *Whitehall.*

> ————*Haec (inquit) limina victor*
> *Alcides subiit, haec illum Regia cepit,*
> *Aude, Hospes, contemnere opes, & te quoque dignum*
> *Finge Deo, rebusque veni non asper egenis.*

(Hercules stooped beneath this threshold; in this cottage the hero
rested. Be brave enough to despise riches. Mould yourself to be
worthy of godhead, and do not despise our poverty.)[29]

Horace is also included in this roster of Classic poets who praise
the merits of agriculture; then, to conclude, Cowley with his
Latin poems on plants places himself in that group.

Vergil, Horace, and Cowley are also represented in the verse
section of *"Of Agriculture."* Cowley translates the conclusion
of *Georgics* II, which emphasizes the quiet modest life of those
whose "low Scene" is laid "in Life's cool vale." Cowley advocates,
as Ben Jonson had in "To Penshurst" and "To Sir Robert Wroth,"
rural simplicity and naturalness as the source of all enduring
personal values. If Cowley's prose essay presents a philosophic
sense of the value of the country life, Vergil's domestic details
elaborate the previous argument:

> This, the young Lamb, that the soft Fleece doth yield,
> This, loads with Hay, and that, with Corn the Field:
> All sorts of Fruit crown the rich *Autumns* Pride:
> And on a swelling Hill's warm stony side,
> The powerful Princely Purple of the Vine,
> Twice dy'd with the redoubled Sun, does shine.
> In th' Evening to a fair ensuing day,
> With joy he sees his Flocks and Kids to play;
> And loaded Kyne about his Cottage stand,
> Inviting with known sound the Milkers hand,
> And when from wholsom labour he doth come,
> With wishes to be there, and wish't for [at] home,
> He meets at door the softest humane blisses,
> His chast Wives welcom, and dear Childrens kisses.[30]

Cowley's next translation (also in heroic couplets) is a part of Horace's popular Epode II, "Beatus ille qui procue. . . ." Partly responsible for the perfection of country life, Horace writes, is its freedom from love—the greatest tyrant of all. Whimsically, he concedes that married happiness is possible, if the wife be "chaste and clean, though homely" and preferably like the girls of his native province, Apulia. The wittier and more urbane selection concludes on the subject of feminine wiles and the advantages of an honest wife; it is apparent that Horace knows the women of the fallen ages of iron and bronze, "Drest by the wanton hand of Luxurie," in the city and court from a point of view not exploited in the selection from Vergil. The Horatian verses, concluding with an explicit contrast between "Princely tables" and those of simple fare,[31] grow more and more sentimentalized and are an excellent introduction to the next selection from Horace's *Satires*, "The Country Mouse."

If Cowley chose the most popular of Horace's Epodes, certainly Satire VI (Book II) is Horace's most popular and accomplished poem in that genre. Perhaps the satires of Book II were, for Cowley, like Montaigne's essays; for their subjects suggest his titles: "On Satire," "On Intelligence," "On Country Life," and so on.[32] Cowley omits the first seventy-eight lines of the satire, concerned with activities in the city and Horace's wish to retire to the lands given him by Maecenas, but he translates the wonderful tale told by Cervius, a country friend of Horace's, of *mus rustica* and *mus urbanus*. This animal fable is about the country mouse who is advised to try the *haute cuisine* of the city and who, frightened by the master's dogs, decides that "This, of all lives (said he) is sure the worst. / Give me again, *ye gods*, my Cave and wood; / With peace, let tares and acorns be my food."[33]

Cowley has succeeded in "paraphrasing" Horace's tone in the wonderful burlesque passages on night and the moon:

> It was the time, when witty Poets tell,
> *That* Phoebus *into* Thetis *bosom fell*:
> *She blusht at first, and then put out the light,*
> *And drew the modest Curtains of the night.*
> Plainly, the troth to tell, the Sun was set.[34]

But witty urbanity and lightness are nowhere better than in the words of the city mouse, who, with boasting and bravado, flatters his country host:

> You should see Towns, and Manners know, and men:
> And taste the generous Lux'ury of the Court,
> Where all the Mice of quality resort;
> Where thousand beauteous shees about you move,
> And by high fare, are plyant made to love.
> We all e're long must render up our breath,
> No cave or hole can shelter us from death.
>   Since Life is so uncertain, and so short,
> Let's spend it all in feasting and in sport.
> Come, worthy Sir, come with me, and partake,
> All the great things that mortals happy make.[35]

The couplets move the reader forward as much as they contain themselves as two-line units. Rhythmically, Cowley succeeds in building up a momentum accented by the colloquial speech patterns and punctuated by the final rhymes. His use of the couplet anticipates Dryden and Pope, while in the translation from Vergil he is still thinking in terms of the long periodic sentence. There, as Walton observes, "the diction maintains an even decorum without colloquialisms or excessive heroic exaggerations. His fancy and judgement are perfectly balanced. . . . The rural scene is 'guilded' and formalized."[36]

Two stylized portraits of rural life and a translation of part of Horace's most popular satire have given the reader different perspectives on the general subject of agriculture. But the subject has been expanded and generalized from the terms of its treatment in the prose essay. There even the practical aspects of farming (the number of years necessary for training in an agricultural college) were discussed along with the philosophical aspects of the subject. The poems offer Cowley an opportunity to illustrate the close relationship between the Classical point of view and his own, and to imply as well a set of values (simplicity, honesty, frugality) inherent in the Classical viewpoint and opposed to those which control life in the city (duplicity, complexity, variety).

Following the Horatian satire on the country mouse, one turns to a third translation from Horace, this example from Book I of the *Epistles*. In the epistle to Fuscus Aristius Horace defends rural liberty to his friend who loves the city; the point is made through the use of an exemplum from the animal world:

> The horned Deer by Nature arm'd so well,
> Did with the Horse in common pasture dwell;

And when they fought, the field it alwayes wan [won],
Till the ambitious Horse begg'd help of Man,
And took the bridle, and thenceforth did reign
Bravely alone, as Lord of all the plain:
But never after could the Rider get
From off his back, or from his mouth the bit.[37]

To gain more than he had by nature, the horse gave up his
liberty to become the slave of man; to gain the riches of the
world, man is willing to give up his personal freedom. Cowley
has reinforced a theme from an earlier essay ("Of Liberty")
and expanded upon the whole question of individual freedom
and its relationships to city and country. To conclude the verse
section of the essay, Cowley adds his own work (in translation,
to be consistent) from Book IV of his Latin poems on plants.
His sentiments are identical with those of Vergil and Horace;
his example of the ideal rural figure is the peasant Agläus, whose
happiness startled the great Gyges (the story is told by Pliny);
and the wishes of his conclusion reflect the happiness of "the
mighty Cowley," who has now "triumphantly retir'd":

So let me act, on such a private stage,
The last dull Scenes of my declining Age;
After long toiles and Voyages in vain,
This quiet Port let my tost Vessel gain,
Of Heavenly rest, this Earnest to me lend,
Let my Life sleep, and learn to love her End.[38]

No other single essay has as many poems following it (about
one-fourth of the poems used in the edition), an obvious indi-
cation of the primary importance of the subject. All the major
themes of the essays are present (they are also developed in
other ways separately): theories of moderation; Renaissance
concepts of the proper regard for oneself and one's freedom;
poetry's association with the pastoral tradition, gardens, and the
Golden Age; the muta persona.

The image perpetuated by Cowley's friend Sprat coincides
with the impression one gains from the final essay. "He had,"
his editor wrote, "a perfect natural goodness, which neither the
uncertainties of his condition nor the largeness of his wit could
pervert. He had a firmness and strength of mind that was of
proof against the Art of Poetry it self."[39] And, as Sprat con-
tinues the eulogy on Cowley's easiness and modesty, his wit,

tenderness, and magnanimity, one can see how such a man must have made a favorable impression on his friends and associates. For a man as humble as Cowley, it was "a hard and nice Subject . . . to write of himself, it grates his own heart to say anything of disparagement, and the Readers Eares to hear any thing of praise from him." Cowley intended to conclude with the essay on himself, but "only in relation to the subject of these precedent discourses";[40] so it is appropriate that he deals both with his early delight in solitude and with his beginnings in poetry. His early natural antipathy to the glories of the world, perhaps encouraged by his youthful acquaintance with Horace, is illustrated by the poem from his teen-age years, "A Vote," from *Sylva* (1636). But reading Spenser made him a poet:

For I remember when I began to read, and to take some pleasure in it, there was wont to lie in my Mothers Parlour (I know not by what accident, for she her self never in her life read any Book but of Devotion) but there was wont to lie *Spencers* Works; this I happened to fall upon, and was infinitely delighted with the Stories of the Knights, and Giants, and Monsters, and brave Houses, which I found every where there: (Though my understanding had little to do with all this) and by degrees with the tinckling of the Rhyme and Dance of the Numbers, so that I think I had read him all over before I was twelve years old, and was thus made a poet. . . .[41]

Then came the university, the Civil War, politics, discouragement, and at last contentment in "Muses, Books, and Liberty and Rest." To follow the pattern of the other essays, he concludes with two translations from Martial and his own "Epitaphium Vivi Auctoris." It is very likely that he thought this concluding essay might be his last work.

III   *"Business which the Muses hate"*

Cowley did not write a great deal of prose; and, excluding the preface to the volume of juvenilia, there are only four additional prose compositions: the Preface to the poems of 1656, *A Proposition for the Advancement of Experimental Philosophy* (1661), *A Discourse by way of Vision, Concerning the Government of Oliver Cromwell* (1661), and the "Preface" to *Cutter of Coleman Street* (1663).

The Preface, earliest of the prose, has its obvious stylistic differences from the essays. The longer periodic sentences and

the more formal tone have greater affinity with Elizabethan
prose than with that of the late seventeenth and eighteenth cen-
turies. Since the volume was prepared while Cowley was im-
prisoned, there is doubtless no little cynicism in his opening
resolution "to make my self absolutely dead in a *Poetical* capa-
city."[42] His intention was "to retire my self to some of our
American Plantations, not to seek for *Gold,* or inrich my self
with the track of those parts. . . . But to forsake this world
for ever, with all the *Vanities* and *Vexations* of it, and to bury
my self there in some obscure retreat. . . ."[43] And, since he
knows that fame comes only posthumously to most poets, he
concludes somewhat sarcastically: "As this therefore is in a true
sense a kind of *Death* to the *Muses,* and a real *literal quitting*
of this *World*: So, methinks, I may make a just claim to the
undoubted priviledge of *Deceased Poets,* which is to be read
with more *favor,* then the Living."[44] Perhaps, as part of the
price for his release from prison, he was ready to forget political
animosities; and his plea to bury party distinctions and past
enmities was grounds for continued suspicion after the Restor-
ation. Two very different prose works belong to the year 1661.
Liek Bacon, Dury, Hartlib, Milton, and Boyle, Cowley published
an essay on educational reforms. *A Proposition for the Advance-
ment of Experimental Philosophy* was written in the winter or
spring of 1659. Sprat's *A History of the Royal Society* considered
Cowley's proposal very important:

While they were thus ord'ring their platform; there came forth a
Treatise, which very much hasten'd its contrivance: and that was a
Proposal by Master *Cowley,* of erecting a Philosophical College. The
intent of it was, that in some place neer *London,* there should liberal
Salaries be bestow'd, on a competent number of Learned Men, to
whom should be committed the operations of Natural Experiments.
This Model was every way practicable; unless perhaps, in two things,
he did more consult the generosity of his own mind, than of other
mens: the one was the *largeness of the Revenue,* with which he would
have his College at first indow'd: the other, that he impos'd on his
Operators, a Second task of great pains, the *Education of youth.*[45]

The researchers of many a university are plagued by precisely
those two qualifications which Bishop Sprat so astutely points
out: the budget and the necessity for large classes. In the Bishop's
mind at least, teaching and research were not compatible; and

these two parts of Cowley's plan may account for the fact that
his college was never realized.

Cowley's wonderfully detailed pamphlet—its exact salary scale
(twenty professors and a chaplain, £120; sixteen apprentice
scholars, £10 for diet, £10 for entertainment; "the four necessary
[cleaning] women ten Pounds") and its precise architectural
and landscaping details—reveals that he had learned well from
Bacon's *Novum Organum* (1620) and *The New Atlantis* (1627?).
Cowley, believing that he could not work within the existing
educational system (few seventeenth-century reformers wanted
anything but their own separate systems and colleges), offered a
plan to cover every aspect of school life.

Future leaders were to be the product of Milton's proposal, "Of
Education," but Cowley had in mind the creation of poets as
well as natural philosophers. Poets ought to know about natural
philosophy, to insure the "truth" of their poetry: "the truth is
we want good Poets (I mean we have but few) who have pur-
posely treated of solid and learned, that is, Natural Matters
(the most part indulging to the weakness of the world, and
feeding it either with the follies of Love, or with the Fables of
gods and Heroes) we conceive that one Book ought to be com-
piled of all the scattered little parcels among the ancient Poets
that might serve for the advancement of Natural Science, and
which would make no small or unuseful or unpleasant Vol-
um[e]."[46] The study of natural sciences was to complement
language study. Languages, as Milton advocated, were to be
put to work immediately; and the students were to learn Latin
and Greek from essential books, not from grammars filled with
rules and precepts.[47]

In spite of the more advanced aspects of Cowley's tract, many
of the names on the reading lists and much of the material
reflect the standard curriculum of Westminster. "Intended,"
Sargeaunt writes, "in some points as an attack upon Busby, the
design still shows Cowley as a Westminster. The College was
to be steeped in Latin. The elements of natural science were to
be studied in Varro and Pliny, the principles of divination in
Cicero. Every month a play of Terence was to walk the boards,
and even the professors' triennial report of their discoveries was
to be written in 'proper and ancient Latin.'"[48] But the great
emphasis on natural sciences and on extensive laboratory space
and areas for experimentation, the division of the school into

four classes instead of six or seven (no elementary subjects were to be taught and students began school at thirteen), and the plan for four members of the faculty to be on a kind of sabbatical leave for three-year periods—"Professors Itinerant," one each in Europe, America, Africa, and Asia—are significantly radical recommendations. The pamphlet indicates a real interest on Cowley's part in the scientific movement of his own age, one which is revealed again in his Latin poems.

The most neglected of his prose compositions may be the most interesting for the casual reader. Published anonymously while Cowley was in France, *The Vision, Concerning the Government of Oliver Cromwell* is incomplete and represents only the first of the three books originally proposed.[49] *"The Second, was to be a Discourse with the Guardian-angel of* England, *concerning all the late Confusions and Misfortunes of it. The Third, to denounce heavy Judgments against the three Kingdoms* [England, Scotland, Ireland] . . . ."[50] Following Cromwell's death, England floundered under the weak guidance of "Richard the Little," while Cowley, watching the disintegration of his country in late 1659 from across the channel, assumed the role of Old Testament prophet on the "Burdens" of the three kingdoms: the army, the divines, the lawyers.[51] To correct whatever impressions anyone might have that Cromwell was in any way a good man, Cowley decided in 1661 to publish his extremely biased Royalist views about the Protector.

The tract is in the form of a dream vision, perhaps, as A. B. Gough notes, to parody "the visions which some of the more fanatical sectaries . . . were accustomed to describe in language and imagery borrowed from the Books of Daniel and Revelation."[52] A verse lament for the chaos and confusion in England is interrupted by the sudden appearance of the antagonist of the drama, "a terrible Apparition," naked and painted "after the manner of the ancient *Britons*"; the triple-crowned Specter holds a bloody sword inscribed with Cromwell's motto, *"Pax quaeritur bello,"* and identifies himself with Cromwell's title, "His Highnesse, the Protector."[53] The specter's panegyric supplies the material for the protagonist's rebuttal throughout the remainder of the essay.

The specter extols Cromwell as the greatest leader the world had ever known and points out the extraordinary fact that the Protector, who had no "eminent qualities of body," was of mean birth and belonged to a family of no particular fortune. His birthright made it all the more surprising that he should attempt what he did, and it was even more unbelievable that such a man should "succeed in so improbable a design." His achievement was no less than the destruction of one of the most powerful European monarchies, literally accomplished by the public execution of the king and by the eventual banishment of the remainder of the royal family and their retainers. But this feat, the speaker points out, was not completely the act of a single man, for it was all done "under the name and wages of a Parliament."

Continuing in catalogue form, the speaker chronicles Cromwell's actions, mentioning, among others, his strength to call, dismiss, create, and destroy numerous parliaments; his military power in conquering England's enemies; his political acumen in maneuvering the many factions of his country; his modesty in refusing to accept either the crown or large sums of public monies as reward for his service. He was, in short, a king without a crown, the perfect savior of his country, a man honored by all men. He left "a name behind him, not to be extinguisht, but with the whole World, which as it is now too little for his praises, so might have been too for his Conquests, if the short line of his Humane Life could have been stretcht out to the extent of his immortal designs."[54]

In the attack which follows, Cowley's speaker distorts in every way the problems, evils, and accomplishments of Cromwell's rule. The number of executions is grossly multiplied, Cromwell's associations with King Charles are presented in an equivocal light, and his attitudes toward kingship and monarchy are misrepresented. Cowley, who is especially vitriolic in his attacks on the Protector's materialism, accuses him of preparing to sell St. Paul's to the Jews for a synagogue, "if their purses and devotions could have reacht to the purpose." He "would have," he slurs, "sold afterwards for as much more St. *Peters* (even at his own *Westminster*) to the Turks for a *Mosquito*."[55] He also accuses Cromwell of doing "sencelesse and fantastical things onely to shew his power of doing or saying any thing," and insidiously he passes on the rumor about Cromwell's alleged comments on the Magna Carta: "It would ill befit mine, or any civil Mouth, to repeat those words which he spoke concerning the most sacred of our *English* Lawes, the Petition of Right, and *Magna Charta*."[56]

The tract is a complete record of a fanatic Royalist view of
Cromwell's career in almost every particular, and at the con-
clusion, the poet is saved by an angelic vision of Charles II
almost as preposterous as the devilish evocation of Cromwell:
"a flash of Light" revealed

> The comeliest Youth of all th' Angelique Race;
> Lovely his shape, ineffable his Face.
> The Frowns with which he strook the trembling Fiend,
> All smiles of Humane Beauty did transcend.[57]

The vision of Charles II "exorcising" the devil Cromwell with
a cross and a few words (one of which was "Jesus") may be one
of the great popaganda scenes of all time; with a melodramatic
gesture, the angel of gold sends off the usurper who "howls as
he goes on."

The final prose essay—chronologically it just precedes the
essays themselves—is the Preface to Cowley's Restoration comedy,
Cutter of Coleman Street (1663). Actually the Preface is a
defense against the charges of those who felt the play was an
attack on the king's party, and perhaps its figures, Colonel Jolly
and the would-be Cavaliers Cutter and Worm, were less burlesque
than one might believe. Some of the many unscrupulous Cavaliers
in London might easily have taken offense at the exaggerated
portraits in the comedy. Cowley defends himself with the tradi-
tional argument: he means not to call professions dishonorable
but to disgrace those who disgrace the professions. Far from
ridiculing Cavaliers, Cowley ridicules those who usurp the name
and title of officer to further their vices. Having explained Colonel
Jolly, Cowley comments on poetic decorum, revealing a point
of view which would certainly rule out some of the great Shake-
spearean comedies, especially *As You Like It*:

*If you be to choose parts for a Comedy out of any noble or elevated
rank of persons, the most proper for that work are the worst of that
kind. Comedy is humble of her Nature, and has alwayes been bred
low, so that she knows not how to behave her self with the great or
the accomplisht. She does not pretend to the brisk and bold Qualities
of Wine, but to the Stomachal Acidity of Vinegar, and therefore is
best placed among that sort of people which the Romans call The
Lees of Romulus. If I had designed here the celebration of the
Virtues of our Friends, I would have made the Scene nobler where
I intended to erect their Statues. They should have stood in Odes,
and Tragedies, and Epique Poems, (neither have I totally omitted*

those greater testimonies of my esteem of them) Sed nunc non erat
hic Locus, &c.[58]

Cowley is still dominated by his schoolboy training in Plautus
and Terence and their low-life "heroes." Defending himself also
against charges of profanity, Cowley reminds his audience that
no one had done more than he *"to root out the ordinary weeds
of Poetry, and to plant it almost wholly with Divinity."*[59] In
conclusion, he realizes that poets' careers have never been easy;
they are always open to attack and misunderstanding. His poig-
nant and beautifully modulated conclusion is in the best tradition
of Cowleyan modesty—and pride—in his dedication to poetry and
to his profession as poet. He thinks that if he had a son who
wished to become a poet, he would probably counsel him against
such a vocation; for, while poets labor to give men delight, there
are always readers who labor equally hard to find offense in
what is written. Poets, he continues, run the risks encountered
by those who express themselves publicly; and, because of the
general ignorance (or maliciousness) of the multitude, they
never achieve the fame they deserve. If their verses are good,
few may recognize their excellence; but, if they are bad, everyone
condemns them. It seems that it is in the nature of the profession
to be maligned, mistreated, and misunderstood.

Intensifying his romantic lament over the poet's plight is
Cowley's recognition that it has always been so for them; none
of the ancient Greek or Roman poets—neither Vergil nor Horace
—escaped this kind of censure, although for these two examples
"the Barkings of a few were drown'd in the Applause of all the
rest of the World, and the Poison of their Bitings extinguisht
by the Antidote of great rewards, and great encouragements."
Such rewards, Cowley admits, he neither expects nor deserves:
"Indolency would serve my turn instead of Pleasure; for though
I comfort my self with some assurance of the favour and affection
of very many candid and good natured (and yet too judicious and
even Critical) persons, yet this I do affirm, that from all which
I have written, I have never received the least benefit, or the
least advantage, but on the contrary have felt sometimes the
effect of Malice and Misfortune."[60]

IV *"God the first Garden made"*

During his retirement from London, Cowley produced not
only the Horatian essays in verse and prose but also six books

of Latin poems, *The History of Plants.* Two of these books were written in the several years immediately preceding their publication in 1662; the final four books were published posthumously in 1668. The poems, which represent Cowley's final literary achievement, are unfortunately available only in A. B. Grosart's collected edition.

Sprat thought of Cowley's Latin poems as the culmination of his career. "He withdrew himself out of the crowd," he wrote,

with desires of enlightening and instructing the minds of those that remain'd in it. It was his resolution in that Station to search into the Secrets of Divine and Humane knowledge, and to communicate what he should observe. He always profess'd that he went out of the world as it was mans, into the same World as it was Natures and as it was Gods. The whole compass of the Creation, and all the wonderful effects of the Divine Wisdom, were the constant Prospect of his Senses and his Thoughts. And indeed he enter'd with great advantage on the studies of Nature, even as the first great Men of Antiquity did, who were generally both Poets and Philosophers. He betook himself to its Contemplation, as well furnish'd with sound Judgment and diligent Observation and good Method to discover its Mysteries, as with Abilities to set it forth in all its Ornaments.[61]

Sprat also contends that in addition to a "Discourse concerning Style," Cowley's final and "principal Design" was a "Review of the Original Principles of the Primitive Church": an examination of "our Saviours and the Apostles lives, and their immediate Successors, for four or five Centuries, till Interest and Policy prevailed over Devotion."[62] When activities in the world of men brought only frustration and disappointment, Cowley turned to observe nature as the source of ultimate value. From nature he would proceed logically up the scale to matters of faith and divinity. In the natural world he hoped to discover the way to the secrets of existence.

Cowley may have thought of the poems on plants as a logical continuation of themes in the *Davideis*. In it he celebrated an Old Testament figure in heroic verse; in the poems on plants his subject was no less divine, for "that which celebrates the wonderful works of Providence [was] not . . . far distant from a sacred poem. Nothing can be found more admirable in Nature than the virtues of several Plants; therefore, amongst other things of a most noble strain, the divine poet upon that account praises the Deity, 'who brings forth grass upon the mountains,

and herbs for the use of man. . . .'"⁶³ In the *Davideis* his mode
was epic; in the poems on plants his manner is also appropriate
to the material: "I propose not here to fly, but only to walk in my
garden, partly for health's sake, and partly for recreation."⁶⁴

In Book I, Cowley's poetical version of a contemporary herbal,
twenty different varieties of herbs, chosen at random, recount
in dialogue to the poet their origins and medicinal qualities;
many repeat the myths associated with their origins and char-
acteristics. Listening patiently to the narrations, the poet begins
to see the place of herbs in the universal order; their qualities
act as beneficial balances for man's infirmities. Hinman observes
that "Cowley's central theme in the first book is the marvelous
fact that for every human ill a living, growing portion of the
universe, a balanced, perpetual process, provides a remedy. Life
is an undiminishing fountain, constantly replenished."⁶⁵ Each of
the herbs, then, has something to do with the preservation of
life. And Cowley succeeds in dramatizing the incidents so that
each herb has its distinct poetic personality. One has, for instance,
the episode of *Mentha* (Mint), whose poignant pleas beg the
listener to discard the "old dubious saws" and "ill conjectures"
about her hospitality to mankind and to accept her as beneficial.
Mint complains that her fame has been maligned by men who
chose to lie about her, and her monologue is a storehouse of
herbal lore and mythology. Men have spread the rumors that
Mint could not be planted in time of war and that, if taken
internally, the leaf made "dull frigid eunuchs" of "brisk men."
She is, she retorts, neither enemy to Mars nor to Venus; for she
is especially capable of improving "the fire of love / With
genial heat"; besides, Mint is an excellent aid for the stomach
and its digestive faculties, a medicinal agent to drain wounds,
and an antidote for the bites of serpents and rabid animals.

Mint is, however, most concerned with the charges that she
is an enemy of Venus; to quell that rumor, she relates (in the
central portion of her monologue) the episode of her meta-
morphosis from maiden to plant, an event directly related to
her "intimacy" with Venus. Pluto, it seems, had fallen in love
with her; and, driven by his lust, he had carried her off to his
secret cave in the underworld. The couple was surprised by
Pluto's consort, Prosperine, who, in her rage, turned the girl
into a plant:

> She no excuse would hear, nor me again
> Let rise; but said, there fix'd I should remain.
> She spake, and straight my body I perceiv'd
> (Each limb dissolv'd) of all it's strength bereav'd:
> My veins are all straight rooted in the earth,
> (From whence my ruddy stalk receives it's birth)
> A blushing crown of flow'rs adorn my head,
> My leaves are jagged, of a darkish red;
> And so a lovely bed of Mint I make
> In the same posture that she did me take.[66]

In pity Pluto bestowed on her leaves their fragrant smell and
their medicinal powers. She serves now, she concludes, to help
maidens grow old and to keep them from the snares set for
her by Pluto. The poem is an example of Cowley's best work
in Book I.

With a mocking dismissal of *Eruca* (Rocket), the herb proud
of its aphrodisiacal powers whose qualities lead men to act out
of order, Cowley begins Book II by indicating that his subject
has to do with the mystery of life itself:

> Cybele's holy mysteries now begin;
> Hence, all you Males! for you it is a sin
> One moment in this hallow'd place to stay,
> You gibing Males![67]

To preside over the "council" of herbs in the Oxford gardens,
Cowley chooses Mugwort; and each herb again recites its par-
ticular qualities—qualities which either assist or abort childbirth,
prevent or hasten menstruation, conception, or lactation. The
first matter for discussion is the

> . . . menstruous source,
> My constant task, 'tis fit we should discourse;
> From what orig'nal spring that Nilus goes,
> Or by what influx it so oft o'reflows;
> What will restrain, and what drive on the tide,
> And what goods or what mischiefs in it glide.[68]

The pageant of this book—an amazing collection of seventeenth-
century gynecological and obstetrical information—includes Pen-
nyroyal, Dittany, Plantain, Rose, Birthwort, the Mastic Tree,
Savin, and Myrrh, each one of whom centers her discussion on
some aspect of the menstural blood, the secret of all life, or on
the whole process of conception and birth. Their claims provide

proof for Cowley of the intimate relationship between man and nature. These natural aids to the mysteries of life assist man in reproducing, and their medicinal effects sustain his health and his life.

Continuing his search into things natural, human, and divine, Cowley moves on in books III and IV to the domain of flowers. In these sections he organizes his material in a way similar to the preceding ones: under pretext of a contest presided over by Flora, who was to choose a Queen of Plants, each flower appears to cite its especial qualifications for the position. In a seasonable pageant, the flowers appear on this morning of May 29 at the side of the Thames; it is the day of the Restoration of Charles II and thus of the re-establishment of domestic order:

> It brought home godlike Charles, and all his peaceful train,
> Compos'd our chaos, cover'd o'er the scars,
> And clos'd the bleeding wounds of twenty years,
> Nor felt the gown about the fruits of peace,
> But gardens, woods, and all the Flow'ry race.
> This year to ev'ry thing fresh honours brought,
> Nor 'midst these were the learned Arts forgot.
> Poor exil'd Flora, with the sylvan gods,
> Came back again to their old lov'd abodes.

This morning is not one for the usual mortal plants to appear; one finds instead the "ideal" flower of each genus:

> But not such Flow'rs as you see growing here,
> Poor mortal Flow'rs, obnoxious still to harms,
> Which quickly die out of their mother's arms,
> But those that Plato saw, Ideas nam'd,
> Daughters of Jove, for heav'nly extract fam'd:
> Ethereal Plants![69]

Earthly plants are only reflections of their ideal in the Creator's mind, but as such they reveal, indirectly, something of God to man.

In the playful lyric, the Tulip makes her bid for the coveted position of queen of plants; the poem is one of Cowley's most delightful. Since Tate's translations, like the Latin originals, are relatively unattainable, the entire poem is cited so the reader may have some clearer idea of the individual monologues:

> Somewhere in Horace, if I don't forget,
> (Flow'rs are no foes to poetry and wit,

For us that tribe the like affection bear,
And of all men the greatest florists are)
We find a wealthy man
Whose wardrobe did five thousand suits contain;
He counted that a vast prodigious store,
But I that number have twice told, and more.
Whate'er in spring the teeming earth commands;
What colours e'er the painted pride of birds,
Or various lights the glist'ring gem affords,
Cut by the artful lipidary's hands;
Whate'er the curtains of the heav'ns can show,
Or light lays dyes upon the varnish'd bow;
Rob'd in as many vests I shine,
In every thing bearing a princely mien.
Pity I must the Lily and the Rose.
(And the last blushes at her threadbard clothes)
Who think themselves so highly bless'd,
Yet have but one poor tatter'd vest.
These studious, unambitious things, in brief,
Would fit extremely well a college-life,
And when the god of Flow'rs a charter grants,
Admission shall be given to these plants:
Kings should have plenty and superfluous store,
Whilst thriftiness becomes the poor.
Hence Spring himself does chiefly me regard:
Will any Flow'r refuse to stand to his award?
Me for whole months he does retain,
And keeps me by him all his reign;
Caress'd by Spring, the season of the year
Which before all to Love is dear.
Besides, the god of Love himself's my friend,
Not for my face alone, but for another end;
Lov'd by the god upon a private score,
I know for what—but say no more.
But why should I
Become silent or so shy?
We Flow'rs were by no peevish fire begot,
Nor from that frigid sullen tree did sprout,
So fam'd in Ceres' sacred rites;
Nor in moroseness Flora's self delights.
My root, like oil in ancient games, prepares
Lovers for battle or those softer wars;
My quick'ning heat their sluggish veins inspires
With vigorous and sprightly fires;

Had but chaste Lucrece us'd the same,
The night before bold Tarquin try'd his flame,
Upon record she ne'er a fool had been,
But would have liv'd to reap the pleasure once again,
The goddess, conscious of the truth, awhile
Contain'd, but then was seen to blush and smile.
The flower-de-luce next loos'd her heav'nly tongue,
And thus, amidst, her sweet companions, sun.[70]

In spite of the idyllic opening, Book III concludes with references to the historical War of the Roses. But Book IV begins with a long Horatian introduction, later translated by Cowley for use in his essay "*Of Agriculture.*" The flowers of summer and autumn are left for lyric discussion, and they are all mentioned early in the book. Again the comments reveal Cowley's exhaustive knowledge of botanical lore. The book concludes in a politic way, as Flora decides like a true Solomon:

Let no one claim what all deserve to have,
....

Rest ever, then, a Commonwealth of Flow'rs,
Compos'd of people and of senators.[71]

She names four Praetors, one to each season: to spring, the Tulip; to summer, the July-flower; to autumn, the Crocus; to winter, the Hellebore. For those who can recognize it, the universe offers an ideal natural kingdom of *utile et dulce.* Cowley's poem both convinces one of that fact and also illustrates it; one has, as Sprat promised, discovered universal mysteries and seen them expressed with best ornament.

The subject expands in Book V to trees, whose fruitfulness dwarfs the usefulness of flowers and herbs. Here the setting is also ideal, for Cowley has chosen to locate his poem in the legendary "Fortunate Isles," where another contest is held, this time between the trees of the old and those of the new worlds. Cowley has the opportunity to list and describe the various bounty given man by the plants which reach to the sky. Out of the quarrel between the new world Omelichilus and his old world counterpart Bacchus (suggestive of the destructive effects of the conquest of the New World by the Old, which sought only gain and plunder), Cowley envisions a type of Hesperian isles where Europeans might live if they could keep their lives in proportion and order. And, he writes in Book VI, that idyll might be realized in England now that Charles II has returned. "The sixth Book," Sprat reports, "is wholly Dedicated to the Honour of his Country. For making the *British* Oak to preside in the Assembly of the Forrest Trees, upon that occasion he enlarges on the History of our late Troubles, the Kings Affliction and Return, and the beginning of the *Dutch* War; and Manages all in a style that (to say all in a word) is equal to the Greatness and Valour of the *English* Nation."[72] That England may still know the golden age she experienced before the Civil War is Cowley's theme for the book which surveys seventeenth-century English history:

> Such was the Golden Age in Saturn's sway;
> Easy and innocent it pass'd away;
> But too much lux'ry and good fortune cloys,
> And virtues she should cherish she destroys.
> What we most wish, what we most toil to gain,
> Enjoyment palls, and turns the bliss to pain.
> Possession makes us shift our happiness
> From peaceful wives to noisy mistresses.
> The repetition makes the pleasure dull;
> 'Tis only Change that's gay and beautiful,
> O notion false! O appetite deprav'd!
> That has the nobler part of man enslav'd:
> Man! born to reason, does that safety quit,
> To split upon the dang'rous rock of wit.
> Physicians say there's no such danger near
> As when, tho' no signs manifest appear,
> Self-tir'd, and dull, man knows not what he ails,
> And without toil his strength and vigour fails.[73]

In spite of regicide, civil war, and attacks from without, the great English oak will remain significant of the order, peace, and stability ultimately possible in Britain. Cowley's final book is a passionate plea to his countrymen to realize in the human commonwealth the ideal fusion of beauty and utility that they may observe in the world of external nature.

CHAPTER 7

"This Pageant of a Prodigie"

I "Who now reads Cowley?"

DISCUSSIONS of Abraham Cowley usually conclude with remarks on Metaphysical poetry and with reference to Dryden and Jonson, the critics responsible for placing Cowley in the seventeenth-century group which "affects the meta-physics."[1] A man who confessed that he did "not know whether it ["Metaphysick"] be any thing or no"[2] may have been surprised to find himself defined and categorized by a term he did not understand. Since few critics agree over its meaning, the term remains without precise definition; arguments continue over whether "Metaphysical" has to do with content, attitude, or technique.[3] The controversy had its modern beginnings in Herbert J. C. Grierson's *Metaphysical Lyrics & Poems of the Seventeenth Century* (1921), while the latest contribution is David Rawlinson's article "Cowley and the Current Status of Metaphysical Poetry" in *Essays in Criticism* (1963).

T. S. Eliot's review of Grierson's important anthology suggests that one avoid the dilemma of "Metaphysical" by pursuing a different method of evaluation. "If so shrewd and sensitive (though so limited) a critic as Johnson," Eliot writes, "failed to define metaphysical poetry by its faults, it is worthwhile to inquire whether we may not have more success by adopting the opposite method; by assuming that the poets of the seventeenth century (up to the Revolution) were the direct and normal development of the precedent age; and, without prejudicing their case by the adjective 'metaphysical,' consider whether their virtue was not something permanently valuable, which subsequently disappeared, but which ought not to have disappeared."[4]

Eliot's suggestion is that one look for the enduring value in Cowley's work rather than emphasize those characteristics which place him in a predetermined group. Such an evaluation can be made only if one looks at all of Cowley's writings, not just the love poems in which he is a conscious follower of the vogue begun in Donne's *Songs and Sonets*. If there were no echoes of Donne, Cowley's poems would not have been successful. The closed couplets of the *Davideis*, the Horatian themes of the essays, and the concerns of *The History of Plants* look forward to Pope and Wordsworth rather than back to Donne. Cowley is a transitional figure, and that makes him important. The ideological values of his work, reflecting as they do many of his age's most notable developments, also make him significant. Critics are beginning to see Cowley with a historical eye, allowing their judgments to involve more than exclusively poetic criteria; the result is that one may read Cowley without condescending to him as an inferior Donne or as a superior Cleveland.

II *"Some honour I would have"*

Historically, it is not difficult to place Cowley's contribution. His *Davideis* is the first "Christian" epic, his Preface the first open argument for converting previously "pagan" poetry to biblical subjects. Milton's great poems—*Samson Agonistes, Paradise Lost, Paradise Regained*—are in the tradition of Cowley's Old Testament epic. To Cowley's popularization of the irregular English "Pindarics" one can trace the odes of Gray, Collins, Wordsworth, Shelley, and others. Addison, Johnson, Lamb, and Hazlitt owe a debt to the essays in verse and prose.

The great theme in all his works, as Robert Hinman's excellent *Abraham Cowley's World of Order* demonstrates, concerns "experimental philosophy" [science]; the poems and prose reveal a significant occupation with the concept of order and with the role of poetry in achieving it. In an age of political and social instability, when the institutions of men were at best expedient and transitory, Cowley looked for order and permanence through art; enduring values were to be established in poetry, the human manifestation of the divine harmony. Poetry imitates

> . . . her Makers Power Divine,
> And changes her sometimes, and sometimes does refine:
> It does, like Grace, the Fallen Tree restore
> To its blest state of Paradise before.[5]

The concept of order in art owes something to Ben Jonson, whose influence on Cowley has not been sufficiently noted.

It is not strange that Cowley has always been seen as the follower of Donne, but one ought to realize that many of Cowley's major ideas about poetry reflect Jonsonian concepts as well. Cowley and Jonson were both interested in what poetry could teach about life and its conduct. Cowley has no set of critical observations in prose such as Jonson's *Timber,* but he too is interested in how poetry mirrors that symmetry and that plan in the universe which are not always apparent to men. Shakespeare's Touchstone thought "the truest poetry is the most feigning"; Cowley and Jonson would have agreed that "truth is truest poesy." To embody in his poetry the clarity, beauty, and simplicity of the universal order was as much Cowley's intention as Jonson's. Eloquence was no substitute for truth, and the "honest" (natural) life advocated in the essays mirrors the poetry produced by a man in such an environment. "Sense," Jonson had written, "is the life and soul of language." And Samuel Johnson had admitted to Boswell that "there is more sense in a line of Cowley than in a page (or a sentence, or ten lines,—I am not quite certain of the very phrase) of Pope."[6]

It would be as misleading to overstate Jonson's influence on Cowley as it has been to exaggerate that of Donne. But one ought to recognize that certain Jonsonian values are important in Cowley's development. Although Cowley does not have Jonson's sophisticated attitude about the relationship between poem and poet revealed in *Timber,* Cowley does evince Jonson's sense of the moral role of poetry and of the responsible position of the poet in the *Davideis* and in *The History of Plants.* Where Jonson favored a study of the poetry and institutions of the ancients, Cowley turned, however, to the natural world itself for enduring analogies of the divine order. Matters of emphasis and technique aside, both poets are aware of the significant relationship of man to his environment.

The mixed strains of Jonson and Donne are obvious in Cowley's work, and he felt their influence so strongly that one finds it difficult to determine what a characteristically Cowleyan idiom is. Not content to sing only with the past, Cowley faced a world whose foundations were changing so rapidly that a new poetic idiom was not sufficiently developed for what he intended to do. "Truth" to Cowley and to Jonson were really very different, for they were found in different places. Jonson looked to the traditions of the past; Cowley, to natural phenomena and to the science of the future. By the time of the *Davideis*, Cowley, caught up in that future world, was attempting to see his hero in terms of contemporary truth. And, as Donne tells one as early as 1611-12, the old truths were crumbling away and there was as yet nothing to replace them. Cowley's very contemporaneity—his desire to speak in the language of the new truths—makes him an exciting figure.

His Muse kept leading him away from the world of men into the world of nature, for to know man, he would start with herbs and flowers. Disappointments in the political world were only partly responsible for his retirement, for he was learning that one can find out more about life by leaving the city than by living in it. Of couse he wasn't always convinced of the truth of that attitude, and he probably could have continued a Cavalier life if had so chosen, but by 1660 he was convinced of the sterility of human endeavor in the world of the court. The secrets of life were to be found in nature herself, and those discoveries were to be the sources of the only enduring happiness—happiness based on truth itself.

Cowley is marked by his own time; to say that is to pay him a great compliment, for he worked and lived on his age's terms. This limitation is his greatest virtue. If his many poetical attempts are not completely successful, the fault is not entirely his. The age of Cowley was not a great one for "modern" verse. Milton, one remembers, is often called the "last Elizabethan," for his great epic is atypical for the latter half of the century. Cowley tried to use in his poems the analogies and metaphors suggested by the changing terms of his own age. To follow his career is to trace many of the intellectual and cultural developments of his own time in a man who felt them sensitively and reflected them in his verse. In the very excitement of novelty and change, Cowley discovered the standards of truth and poetry in his own age; and he refused to look back to a greater, more stable era for his model. To read his work is not simply an exercise in literary history; it is to experience, and rediscover along with the poet, something of the excitement of Cowley's own times.

Notes and References

Chapter One

1. Thomas Sprat, "*An Account of the Life and Writings of Mr. Abraham Cowley . . .*," ed. J. E. Spingarn, *Critical Essays of the Seventeenth Century* (Bloomington, 1957), II, 121.

2. Anthony à Wood recognized Vaughan's error (*Fasti Oxonienses* [London, 1721], II, col. 120). Had Vaughan prepared the engraving several years earlier? (See Arthur H. Nethercot, *Abraham Cowley, The Muse's Hannibal* [Oxford, 1931], p. 22). *A Transcript of the Registers of the Company of Stationers of London* (London, 1875-77) is quite clear about the entry date of October 24, 1632: "a Booke called *Poeticall blossomes conteyning the tragicall* stories of 'CONSTANTIA and PHILETUS' and 'PIRAMUS and THISBE'" (IV, 261).

3. "To the Reader," *Abraham Cowley: Essays, Plays and Sundry Verses*, ed. A. R. Waller (Cambridge, Eng., 1906), p. 3. Subsequent references cite this edition as Volume II of *Works*. Wood errs when he states that one of the poems in the little book was "Antonius and Melida" (*Fasti*, II, col. 120).

4. Sprat, "Account," II, 121.

5. *Works*, II, 15; 16; 17; 20.

6. *Ibid.*, pp. 7, 8, 9.

7. *Ibid.*, p. 10.

8. *Ibid.*, p. 11.

9. "Cowley may well have read Ovid in Latin," writes Douglas Bush, "but he was more familiar with Golding than perhaps his 'very loving Master' of Westminster would have thought desirable. In fact, he sometimes follows Golding when Golding does not follow Ovid" (*Mythology and the Renaissance Tradition in English Poetry*, new rev. ed. [New York, 1963], p. 203).

10. *Works*, II, 32.

11. *Ibid.*, p. 35.

12. *Ibid.*, p. 39.

13. See, e.g., I, v, 46 ("A ruefull sight, as could be seene with eie") and II, vii, 22 ("On thother side in one consort there sate") from *The Faerie Queene* in *The Works of Edmund Spenser*, ed. Edwin Greenlaw *et al.* (Baltimore, 1932-57), I, 67; II, 83.

14. See "*Of My self*," *Works*, II, 457.

15. *Spenser's Minor Poems,* ed. Ernest de Sélincourt (Oxford, 1960), p. 113. See also *The Faerie Queene,* IV, x, 23:

> In such luxurious plentie of all pleasure,
> It seem'd a second paradise to ghesse,
> So lavishly enricht with natures treasure,
> That if the happie soules, which doe possesse,
> Th' *Elysian fields* and live in lasting blisse. . . .

16. *Works,* II, 42-43.

17. Arthur Nethercot makes the same suggestion (*Abraham Cowley,* pp. 19-20).

18. *Works,* II, 48. The lines may be paraphrased as follows: "While citing culprits in atrocious Latin, the judge imposes enormous fines."

19. *Ibid.,* p. 50.

20. The translation of Ode XXIX from Book III is by Joseph P. Clancy, *The Odes and Epodes of Horace* (Chicago, 1960), p. 152. The original is as follows:

> Ille potens sui
> Laetusque deget, cui licet in diem
> Dixisse, 'Vixi: cras vel atra
> Nube polum pater occupato
>
> Vel sole puro; non tamen inritum
> Quodcumque retrost efficiet, neque
> Diffinget infectumque reddet
> Quod fugiens semel hora vexit.'

See *Horace: Odes and Epodes,* ed. Paul Shorey, rev. Paul Shorey and Gordon J. Laing (Chicago and New York, 1919), p. 92.

21. Robert Shafer, *The English Ode to 1660* (Princeton, 1918), p. 126.

22. Nethercot, *Abraham Cowley,* p. 28.

23. *Works,* II, 51.

24. See the discussion in Shafer, *The English Ode,* pp. 123-28.

25. The translation was completed years before its publication in 1640.

26. Shafer, *The English Ode,* p. 124, points to Ode XII (Book I), Ode XXX (Book III), and Ode VIII (Book IV).

27. *Works,* II, 60.

28. See Horace's Ode XVI (Book II) and Ode XVI (Book III) in Shorey and Laing, *Horace,* pp. 50-51, 78-79.

29. *Works,* II, 61.

30. *Ibid.,* p. 62. Compare this attitude with that in Jonson's popular songs from *The Silent Woman* (1609):

> *Still to be neat, still to be drest,*
> *As, you were going to a feast;*
> *Still to be pou'dred, still perfum'd:*
> *Lady, it is to be presum'd,*
> *Though arts hid causes are not found,*
> *All is not sweet, all is not sound,*
> *Giue me a looke, giue me a face,*
> *That makes simplicitie a grace;*
> *Robes loosely flowing, haire as free:*
> *Such sweet neglect more taketh me,*
> *Then all th'adulteries of art.*
> *They strike mine eyes, but not my heart.*

(*Works,* ed. C. H. Herford and Percy Simpson [Oxford, 1925-52], V, 167).

31. For parallels in subject matter, cf. Horace's Ode XXXV (Book I), Ode XVI (Book II) in Shorey and Laing, *Horace,* pp. 30-32; 50-51. Cf. also Satire VI (Book II) in *Satiren,* ed. Adolf Kiessling, rev. Richard Heinze (Berlin, 1961), pp. 296-318.

32. *Works,* II, 66.

33. The title page informs us it was written "At the time of his being Kings Scholler in *West-minster* Schoole" (*ibid.,* p. 67).

34. *Ibid.,* p. 71.

35. *Ibid.,* pp. 88-89.

36. "Abraham Cowley," *Seventeenth Century Studies: A Contribution to the History of English Poetry* (London, 1883), p. 179.

37. *Abraham Cowley,* p. 34. Johnson makes no evaluative comment on the play; see his "Cowley," *Lives of the English Poets,* ed. George Birkbeck Hill (Oxford, 1905), I, 4.

38. "Cowley," *Seventeenth Century Studies,* p. 179.

39. W. W. Greg, *Pastoral Poetry and Pastoral Drama* (London, 1906), p. 365.

40. A. H. Nethercot, "Abraham Cowley as Dramatist," *Review of English Studies,* IV (1928), 5.

41. Greg, *Pastoral Poetry and Pastoral Drama,* p. 362.

42. Nethercot, "Cowley as Dramatist," p. 4.

43. John Genest, *Some Account of the English Stage* (Bath, 1832), X, 64.

44. Nethercot, "Abraham Cowley as Dramatist," pp. 8-16.

45. Samuel Johnson, "Cowley," I, 4.

46. *The Diary of Samuel Pepys,* ed. Henry B. Wheatley (New York, 1946), I, 236.

47. *Poems,* ed. A. R. Waller (Cambridge, Eng., 1905), p. 5. Subsequent references will cite this edition as Volume I of *Works.*

48. *Works* II, 161.

49. *Ibid.*, p. 217.

50. *Ibid.*, p. 220.

51. *Ibid.*, p. 231.

52. *Ibid.*, pp. 189-90.

Chapter Two

1. *Works,* I, 9-10.

2. To that same time at Cambridge probably belong the anti-scholastical poems *"The Tree of Knowledge. That there is no Knowledge. Against the Dogmatists"* and *"Reason: The use of it in* Divine Matters" (*Ibid.*, pp. 45-47).

3. Nethercot, *Abraham Cowley,* p. 48.

4. See William G. Crane, *Wit and Rhetoric in the Renaissance* (New York, 1937), *passim.*

5. *"A Discourse upon Gondibert, An Heroick Poem,"* Spingarn, *Essays,* II, 21-22.

6. *Ibid.*, p. 20.

7. Austin Warren, *Richard Crashaw: A Study in Baroque Sensibility* (University, La., 1939), p. 75.

8. Scott Elledge, "Cowley's Ode 'Of Wit' and Longinus on the Sublime: A Study of One Definition of the Word 'Wit,'" *Modern Language Quarterly,* IX (1948), 185-98.

9. George Williamson writes: "Besides this art of analysis in Cowley, there is the rational evolution, the lyric argument, which comes from Donne. Such intellectual structure is found in the poems of Cowley as diverse as *The Change* and *Of Wit"* (*The Donne Tradition: A Study in English Poetry from Donne to the Death of Cowley* [Cambridge, Mass., 1930], p. 183).

10. We do not know to whom the poem is addressed, but A. H. Nethercot guesses it was to William Hervey: "Whom could the final stanza fit but Hervey?" (*Abraham Cowley,* p. 47). The guess is, however, circumstantial and without external or conclusive internal evidence.

11. See Cowley's ode, "Here's to thee, Dick," in *Works,* I, 26.

12. The point is made by Harvey D. Goldstein in his unpublished doctoral dissertation (Northwestern, 1960), "Cowley and the Pindarick Madness," p. 84. Goldstein has an excellent treatise on wit and its seventeenth-century traditions and a detailed discussion of the ode. My reading is indebted to Mr. Goldstein's analysis. Cf. Robert Hinman's reading (*Abraham Cowley's World of Order* [Cambridge, Mass., 1960], pp. 124-29).

13. *Works,* I, 18.

14. See Goldstein's demonstration, "Cowley and the Pindarick Madness," pp. 80-90.

15. "Cowley," I, 36.

16. Nethercot, *Abraham Cowley*, p. 67.

17. *Works*, I, 25.

18. William Hervey was the first cousin of Henry, Lord Jermyn, who was later to employ Cowley as his private secretary.

19. *Works*, I, 33.

20. *Ibid.*, p. 34.

21. *Works*, ed. E. V. Lucas (London, 1903), V, 284. Cf. Johnson's opinion: "In his poem on the death of Hervey there is much praise, but little passion, a very just and ample delineation of such virtues as a studious privacy admits, and such intellectual excellence as a mind not yet called forth to action can display. He knew how to distinguish and how to commend the qualities of his companion, but when he wishes to make us weep he forgets to weep himself, and diverts his sorrow by imagining how his crown of bays, if he had it, would *crackle* in the *fire*. It is the odd fate of this thought to be worse for being true. The bay-leaf crackles remarkably as it burns; as therefore this property was not assigned it by chance, the mind must be thought sufficiently at ease that could attend to such minuteness of physiology. But the power of Cowley is not so much to move the affections, as to exercise the understanding" ("Cowley," I, 36-37).

22. See J. J. Cohane's article on the stanzaic pattern and the possibility that Yeats's use of a similar stanza in "Byzantium" and other poems reveals some influence by Cowley ("Cowley and Yeats," *Times Literary Supplement* [May 10, 1957], p. 289).

23. *Abraham Cowley: sa Vie, son Oeuvre* (Paris, 1931), p. 499. The original is as follows: ". . . avec ses oppositiones symétriques de termes, donne à son vers un relief de médaille. À l'énergie et à la clarté se joint l'harmonie de balancement. Ainsi s'affirme, dans les caractères généraux du style de Cowley, la tendance oratoire et intellectuelle de sa poésie. La pensée y prend le pas sur le sentiment, l'éloquence remplace le lyrisme. . . ."

24. *Works*, II, 37.

25. *Ibid.*, pp. 42-43.

26. Spingarn, *Essays*, I, 191.

27. The incomplete chivalric romance is set in Lombardy in the court of King Aribert. Rhodalind, the king's daughter (wooed by Prince Oswald), loves Gondibert, who is attracted to Birtha. Oswald's attempts to eliminate Gondibert conclude the portion Davenant finished.

28. Douglas Bush, *English Literature in the Earlier Seventeenth Century*, 2nd ed. (Oxford, 1962), p. 373.

29. His ship was taken by the enemy, and he was imprisoned in the Tower of London from 1650 to 1652.

30. Samuel Johnson, "Cowley," I, 39.

31. See the biographical sketch of Richard Crashaw in L. C. Martin, ed., *Poems* (Oxford, 1927), pp. xv-xxxviii.

32. *Ibid.*, pp. 220-21.

33. Wood reports that Crashaw "was for a time put to his shifts . . . [and] took up his abode for a time in the great city of Paris; But being a meer Scholar and very Shiftless, Mr. *Abr. Cowley* the Poet, did, upon intimation of his being there, find him out in a very sorry condition, *An.* 1646, or thereabouts" (*Fasti,* II, col. 3).

34. *Works,* I, 48-49.

35. Geoffrey Walton, *From Metaphysical to Augustan* (London, 1955), p. 52.

36. *Seventeenth Century Studies,* p. 190.

37. "Cowley," I, 39.

38. *Works,* II, 57. See Thomas Stanley's translation in *Works,* ed. Galbraith Miller Crump (Oxford, 1962), p. 94; and Lovelace's poem in *Works,* ed. C. H. Wilkinson (Oxford, 1930), pp. 38-40.

39. *Works,* II, 55. Stanley's version is in *Works,* pp. 95-96.

40. *Works,* II, 50.

41. *Ibid.*, p. 53.

42. The phrase is Johnson's ("Cowley," I, 40).

43. *Works,* II, 55-56.

44. Johnson's opinion seems definitive on *"The Chronicle"*: "The *Chronicle* is a composition unrivalled and alone: such gaiety of fancy, such facility of expression, such varied similitude, such a succession of images, and such a dance of words, it is vain to expect except from Cowley. His strength always appears in his agility, his volatility is not the flutter of a light, but the bound of an elastick mind. His levity never leaves his learning behind it; the moralist, the politician, and the critick, mingle their influence even in this airy frolick of genius. To such a performance Suckling could have brought the gaiety, but not the knowledge; Dryden could have supplied the knowledge, but not the gaiety" ("Cowley," I, 37-38).

45. *Works,* II, 39-42.

46. As A. H. Nethercot has commented, "A great many of these names are identifiable with persons in one way or another connected with the author's life or works. Here are Katherine, Andria, and Thomasine—Cowley's two sisters and his mother. Here is Elisa— and among the juvenilia published after his death is a song to 'Elisa' . . . Here is Ann—and Cowley had published a poem to Mrs. Anne Whitfield in his juvenilia. Catherine, Susanna, and Isabella

are named—and these were the names of Van Dyke's three sisters. A 'gentle Henrietta' and a 'Mary' are named together—and Cowley was in the court of Henrietta Maria" (*Abraham Cowley*, p. 109).

47. *Works*, I, 41.

Chapter Three

1. The printer's remarks to the reader imply that the edition was not supervised or approved by the poet: "*A Correct Copy of these verses (as I am told) written by the Authour himselfe, falling into my hands, I thought fit to send them to the Presse; Chiefely because I heare that the same is like to be don from a more imperfect one. It is not my good fortune to bee acquainted with the Authour any farther then his fame (by which hee is well knowne to all English men) and to that I am sure I shall doe a service by this Publication: Not doubting but that, if these verses please his Mistresse but halfe so well as they will generally doe the rest of the world, he will be so well contended, as to forgive at least this my boldnesse, which proceedes onely from my Love of him . . .*" (*Works*, I, 456).

The texts of the three major editions of these poems—the "unauthorized" of 1647 (A), Cowley's supervised edition of 1656 (B), and the first posthumous edition of 1668 (C)—are substantially identical. John Sparrow's study concludes that there is a direct linear relationship between the versions: "the text of B was set up from a copy of A, and that of C from a copy of B" ("The Text of Cowley's *Mistress*," *Review of English Studies*, III [1927], 24). The textual relationship suggests that Cowley may have indeed supplied the manuscript for the 1647 edition; if he depended upon it in 1656 it must have been fairly accurate.

2. "*The Given Love*," *Works*, I, 70.

3. *Ibid.*, p. 10. The Latin quotation is from Vergil's *Georgics*, III, 244, where he speaks of sexual passion among animals. All, including man, "rush to this fiery madness: love is alike for all" (*The Eclogues and Georgics of Virgil*, trans. C. Day Lewis [Anchor Books, 1964], p. 173).

4. *Ibid.*

5. See Edmund Elys' *An Exclamation to All those that Love the Lord Jesus in Sincerity, Against An Apology Written by an Ingenious Person, for Mr. Cowley's Lascivious and Profane Verses* (London, 1670).

6. Samuel Johnson, "Cowley," I, 6-7.

7. *Works*, II, 429.

8. *Anacreon Tius, Poeta Lyricus, Summa Cura et Diligentia ad Fidem Etiam, Vet. Ms. Vaticani* (Cantabrigiae, 1705), p. 32.

9. Joseph Spence, *Anecdotes, Observations, and Characters,* ed. S. W. Singer (London, 1820).

10. *Ibid.,* pp. 285-86.

11. *Abraham Cowley,* p. 103.

12. "The Gazers," "The Incurable," "Honour," "The Innocent Ill," "DIALOGUE," "Verses lost upon a Wager," and "Bathing in the River" are the additions.

13. *Works,* I, 147.

14. *Ibid.,* p. 148.

15. "Answer to the Platonicks," *ibid.,* pp. 80-81.

16. *Works,* I, 75-76.

17. *The Mistress, with other Select Poems of Abraham Cowley* (1618-1667) (London, 1926), p. xvi.

18. *Ibid.*

19. *Works,* I, 129.

20. *Ibid.,* p. 133.

21. A. H. Nethercot calls attention to this disunity: "In 'Love Given Over,' the 'wretched Cowley' admits to having wasted three of his 'lustiest' and 'freshest' years in his luckless pursuit, but in other poems periods of five years or one year are mentioned. Nor do the lyrics seem to belong to the same stratum of his work. 'Against Hope' and 'For Hope,' for example, had already been printed in 1646 by Humphrey Moseley, Cowley's new publisher. . . . Similarly, 'The Motto,' an early poem, later removed to another section of Cowley's works, first appeared as a postscript to *The Mistress*" (*Abraham Cowley,* p. 104).

22. Loiseau, *Abraham Cowley,* p. 368. The French text is as follows: "Le poète ne veut y prendre acune initiative. Il se cantonne résolument dans la tradition, et se prépare à grossir d'une unité la longue théorie des poètes qui, à la suite de Pétrarque, chantent les tortures délicieuses de l'amour."

23. *Works,* I, 108-09.

24. Loiseau, *Abraham Cowley,* p. 380.

25. *Works,* I, 91-92.

26. *Ibid.,* pp. 93-94.

27. *Ibid.,* pp. 101-02.

28. "A Discourse Concerning the Original and Progress of Satire," *Of Dramatic Poesy and Other Critical Essays,* ed. George Watson (London, 1962), II, 76.

29. See Leonard Nathanson, "The Context of Dryden's Criticism of Donne's and Cowley's Love Poetry," *Notes and Queries,* CCII (1956), 56-59.

30. "Cowley," I, 40-41; 42.

31. "Cowley," *Seventeenth Century Studies,* p. 184.

32. See the chapter on Metaphysical poetry in Walton's *Metaphysical to Augustan,* pp. 58-64.

33. The case for *The Mistress* as a series of satiric poems is made by Lou Baker Noll, "Abraham Cowley's Lyric Achievement," unpublished doctoral dissertation (Colorado, 1959). Noll claims that Cowley "ingeniously used the manners of metaphysical love poetry to satirize its own attitudes and devices" (p. 2).

34. *Seventeenth-Century English Literature* (New York, 1961), p. 71.

Chapter Four

1. Jean Loiseau, *Abraham Cowley's Reputation in England* (Paris, 1931), *passim.* See the section of Thomas Flatman's stanza from his *"To my Reverend Friend, Dr. Sam. Woodford, On his Excellent Version of the Psalms. Pindaric Ode,"* in *Minor Poets of the Caroline Period,* ed. George Saintsbury (Oxford, 1921), III, 306:

> Bold man, that dares attempt Pindaric now,
> Since the great Pindar's greatest Son
> From the ingrateful age is gone;
> Cowley has bid the ingrateful age adieu;
> Apollo's rare Columbus, he
> Found out new worlds of Poesy:
> He, like an eagle, soar'd aloft,
> To seize his noble prey;
> Yet as a dove's, his soul was soft,
> Quiet as Night, but bright as Day:
> To Heaven in a fiery chariot He
> Ascended by seraphic Poetry;
> Yet which of us dull mortals since can find
> Any inspiring mantle, that he left behind?

See also the stanza from Thomas Sprat's praise of Cowley:

> Thy high Pindarics soar
> So high, where never any wing till now could get;
> And yet thy wit
> Doth seem so great, as those that do fly lower.
> Thou stand'st on Pinadr's back;
> And therefore thou a higher flight dost take:
> Only thou art the eagle, he the wren,
> Thou hast brought him from the dust,
> And made him live again.

Pindar has left his barbarous Greece, and thinks
it just
To be led by thee to the English shore;
An honour to him: Alexander did no more,
Nor scarce so much, when he did save his house before,
When his word did assuage
A warlike army's violent rage:
Thou hast given to his name,
Than that great conqueror sav'd him from a
brighter flame.
He only left some walls where Pindar's name might stay,
Which with time and age decay:
But thou hast made him once again to live;
Thou didst to him new life and breathing give.
And, as in the last resurrection,
Thou hast made him rise more glorious, and put on
More majesty; a greater soul is given to him, by you,
Than ever he in happy Thebes or Greece could shew.

("Upon the Poems of the *English Ovid, Anacreon, Pindar, and Vergil*, Abraham Cowley, In Imitation of His Own Pindaric Odes" in *The Works of the English Poets* . . ., ed. Alexander Chalmers [London, 1810], IX, 328). There are discussions of the odes by Walton, *Metaphysical to Augustan*, pp. 75-94; by Shafer, *The English Ode*, pp. 123-57; and by George N. Shuster, *The English Ode from Milton to Keats* (New York, 1940), pp. 94-123.

2. Sprat, "Account," II, 131.

3. Ben Jonson had included a Pindaric in *Under-Wood* (1616), "To the Immortal Memorie, and Friendship of that Noble Paire, Sir Lucius Cary and Sir H. Morison," but he followed Pindar's three-part division: "turn," "counter-turn," and "stand."

4. Thomas Sprat, "Account," II, 132.

5. A. H. Nethercot, "The Relation of Cowley's 'Pindarics' to Pindar's Odes," *MP*, XIX (1921), 107-9.

6. John Dryden, "The Preface to Ovid's *Epistles*," *Of Dramatic Poesy and Other Critical Essays*, ed. George Watson (London, 1962), I, 268. The musical phrase means "variations on a theme."

7. *Works*, I, 155.

8. *Ibid.*

9. Dryden, "Preface to Ovid's *Epistles*," I, 270-71.

10. *Works*, I, 156.

11. *Ibid.*, pp. 161-62.

12. *Ibid.*, p. 168.

13. *Ibid.*, p. 157.

14. *Ibid.*, p. 162.

15. Cowley, who renders only the first part of Horace's ode, omits the celebration of the victories of Emperor Augustus.

16. *Works*, I, 180.

17. *Ibid.*, p. 178.

18. *Ibid.*, pp. 178-79. Sprat called attention to the appropriateness of the Pindaric "for all manner of subjects: For the Pleasant, the Grave, the Amorous, the Heroic, the Philosophical, the Moral, the Divine" ("Account," II, 132).

19. *Works*, I, 179.

20. *Ibid.*, p. 183.

21. *Ibid.*

22. *Ibid.*, p. 185.

23. *Ibid.*, p. 187.

24. *Ibid.*

25. *Ibid.*, p. 186.

26. Abraham Cowley, p. 116. See Hinman's fine reading of the ode, *Abraham Cowley*, pp. 111-16.

27. See the anonymous, vitriolic answer to Cowley's poem (the two poems are printed side by side for comparison), in the volume *The True Effigies of the Monster of Malmesbury: Or, Thomas Hobbes in his Proper Colours* (London, 1680); the poem is entitled, "Mr. *Cowley's* Verses in Praise of Mr. Hobbes, Oppos'd, By a Lover of Truth." As a sample, here is the "answer" to the stanza quoted in my text:

> His Monstrous Thoughts may well be call'd *Gigantick Sense*,
>> To Heaven they fain would offer *violence*,
>>> Like those *Giants* of old
>>> Of which the *Poets* told.
>> Even like *Goliath* they *Defie*
> The *Armies of the Living God*, and like him too they *Die*.
> The man with his *Gigantic Sense*, his mighty *Spear* and *Shield*
>> Comes forth into the Field;
>> And for some time he Boasted there
>> As if he had no Cause to Fear.
>> *His* Captive-Darkned *Soul cann't see,*
>> *What 'tis to have our Souls set free*
> *From the Black Chains of dire* NECESSITIE:
>> This and a Thousand Errors more
>> He strives to *Land* upon our Shoar;
> But then the Mighty BRAMHAL comes, and takes his Arms away,
>> Shews that this *Painted Shield's not fit for Fight, but Play,*
> Strikes down the Monster, doth to All his *Ugly Shape* display.

Then in another Field he's met by th'Mighty WARD;
And here 'twas plainly seen, that he could neither guard
            Himself from being Wounded, or give Wounds;
            Down strait he falls, his Armour on him sounds,
What e're his Followers say, he never Rose again:
His *Ghost* is heard to Rave sometimes, but then Bold TOM was slain.

28. *Works,* I, 189-90.

29. See Hinman's discussion, to which I am indebted, of the philosophical background of the ode (*Abraham Cowley,* pp. 92-93; 159-62).

30. *Works,* I, 196.

31. *Ibid.,* p. 201.

32. *Ibid.,* p. 199.

33. The eleven eight-line stanzas rhyme abbaccdd; the line lengths are irregular.

34. *Works,* I, 194.

35. *Ibid.,* pp. 193-94.

36. *Ibid.,* p. 203.

37. *Ibid.,* p. 208.

38. *Ibid.,* p. 214.

39. *Ibid.*

40. *Ibid.,* p. 224.

41. Geoffrey Walton, *Metaphysical to Augustan,* p. 83.

Chapter Five

1. "Preface," *A Paraphrase Upon the Psalms of David* (London, 1667), as cited in Loiseau, *Abraham Cowley's Reputation in England,* p. 38.

2. Spingarn, II, 171. Rhymer's discussion, however, continues with criticism unfavorable to the poem.

3. "The Preface, Being an Essay on Heroic Poetry," *The Augustan Reprint Society,* No. 2 (London, 1947). This reprint is that of the second edition (1697).

4. "Account," II, 133.

5. *Seventeenth Century Studies,* p. 195.

6. *Paradise Lost and the Seventeenth Century Reader,* 2nd ed. (London, 1962), p. 122.

7. *Seventeenth-Century English Poetry,* p. 116. The reference is to Cowley's version of the creation, but it seems fair to generalize the remark.

8. *English Poetry in the Earlier Seventeenth Century,* p. 376. See also the statistics presented by J. L. McBryde Jr., "A Study of

Cowley's *Davideis,"* *Journal of English and Germanic Philology,* II (1900), 454-527; III (1901), 24-35.

9. Samuel Johnson, "Cowley," I, 53.

10. *Ibid.,* p. 55.

11. Thomas Sprat, "Account," II, 132-33.

12. A. H. Nethercot, *Abraham Cowley,* pp. 57-58. Frank Kermode points out that the probable source of the poem's neo-Platonism is Kircher's *Musurgia Universalis,* which was not published until 1650 in Rome ("The Date of Cowley's *Davideis,"* *Review of English Studies,* XXV [1949], 156).

13. *The Letters of Dorothy Osborne to William Temple,* ed. G. C. Moore Smith (Oxford, 1928), pp. 169-70.

14. Cowley was impressed with the *precieux coterie* of Katherine Phillips and (like John Keats) was also won over by her poetry, which he celebrated in his ode to her charms and abilities; the ode, which served as a commendatory poem to an unauthorized edition of her poems in 1664, praised her "well knit sense,"

> Thy numbers gentle, and thy fancies high,
> Those as thy forehead smooth, these sparkling as thine eye.
> > 'Tis solid, and 'tis manly all,
> > Or rather, 'tis angelical:
> > > For, as in Angels, we
> > > Do in thy verses see
> Both improv'd sexes eminently meet;
> They are than Man more strong, and more than Woman sweet.

(*Minor Poets of the Caroline Period,* ed. George Saintsbury [Oxford, 1905], I, 496). A delightful account of her circle (of which Cowley was undoubtedly a member)—"Lucasia" (Anne Owen), "Rosania" (Mary Aubrey), "Regina" (Mrs. John Collier), "Valeria" (Lady Anne Boyle), "noble Palaemon" (Jeremy Taylor), "Poliarchus" (Sir Charles Cotterel), and many others—is given by Edmund Gosse in "The Matchless Orinda," *Seventeenth Century Studies,* pp. 203-30). One of her poems, "Upon the Engraving of her Name upon a Tree in Barn-Elms Walks," indicates that she may have visited Cowley before she died; Cowley's elegy, "On the death of Mrs. Katherine Phillips," celebrates in Pindaric form her wit, beauty, and accomplishments.

15. *Abraham Cowley,* pp. 166-67.

16. Kermode, "The Date of Cowley's *Davideis,"* p. 157.

17. *Works,* I, 11.

18. *Ibid.,* p. 12.

19. "A Discourse Upon *Gondibert,"* Spingarn, II, 32.

20. The lines are from Vergil's *Georgics,* II, 457-78.

21. *Works*, I, 13.

22. "A Discourse Upon *Gondibert*," Spingarn, II, 32.

23. *Works*, I, 13-14.

24. *Ibid.*, p. 14.

25. *Ibid.*, p. 269.

26. *Ibid.*, p. 273.

27. "The number of years from *Benjamin* to *Sauls* reign [800]; not exactly: but this is the next *whole number*, and *Poetry* will not admit of broken ones: and indeed, though it were in prose, in so passionate a speech it were not natural to be punctual" (*Ibid.*, p. 272). "They were 33 [text reads "Twice fifteen"] but *Poetry* instead of the broken number, chuses the next entire one, whether it be more or less then the truth" (*Ibid.*, p. 360).

28. "There is great caution to be used in English in the placing of *Adjectives* (as here) after their *Substantives*. I think when they constitute specifical *differences* of the *Substantives*, they follow best; for then they are to it like *Cognomina* or *Surnames* to *Names*, and we must not say, the *great Pompey* or the *Happy Scylla*, but *Pompey the Great*, and *Scylla the Happy*; sometimes even in other cases the *Epithete* is put last very gracefully of which a good *ear* must be the *Judge* for ought I know, without any *Rule*. I chuse rather to say *Light Divine*, and *Command Divine*, then *Divine Light* and *Divine Command*" (*Ibid.*, p. 307).

29. *Ibid.*, p. 321.

30. *Ibid.*, II, 351.

31. "A Discourse Upon *Gondibert*," Spingarn, II, 11.

32. "Answer to Davenant," *Ibid.*, p. 62.

33. *Works*, I, 243.

34. *Ibid.*, p. 246.

35. See the fine discussion in Isabel G. MacCaffrey's *Paradise Lost as "Myth"* (Cambridge, Mass., 1959), pp. 44-119.

36. *Works*, I, 244.

37. *Ibid.*, p. 251.

38. *Ibid.*, p. 244.

39. *Ibid.*, pp. 250-51.

40. *Ibid.*, pp. 253.

41. Orpheus, Cowley's note tells us, "is said to have formed an Harp with four strings, and set them to different Tunes: The first to *Hypate*, to answer to the *Fire*. The second to *Parhypate*, for the *Water*. The third to *Paranete*, for the *Air*. And the fourth to *Nete*, for the *Earth*" (*Ibid.*, p. 276).

42. *Ibid.*, p. 253.

43. *Ibid.*, p. 254.

44. *Ibid.*, p. 259.

45. *Ibid.*, p. 264.
46. *Ibid.*, p. 286.
47. *Ibid.*
48. *Ibid.*, p. 308.
49. *Ibid.*, p. 295.
50. *Ibid.*, p. 305.
51. Hobbes, "Answer to Davenant," Spingarn, II, 62.
52. *Works*, I, 331.
53. *Ibid.*, p. 332.
54. *Ibid.*, p. 343.
55. *Ibid.*, p. 344.
56. *Ibid.*, pp. 371-72.
57. *Ibid.*, p. 372.
58. *Ibid.*, p. 396.

Chapter Six

1. *Works*, I, 455.
2. "Account," II, 125.
3. See the exchange of letters edited by C. H. Firth in *The Academy*, MCXVIII (1893), 296.
4. "I cannot forbeare to tell you of an imprudent discourse that ye last weeke came from one that pretends to witt, but might very well haue more discretion or loyalty, viz. Sir W^m. Davenant. Hee being in company with two *Parliament men and a confident of Monke,* discoursing of *the King and composing* of differ*ences,* told a story of *how the King would not let M^r. Cooley kisse his hand,* though sollicited and presented by *Lo. Jermin,* which argues *irreconcileablenesse in his naturè,* as if inferd by ye company, and *for the Kings dis*aduantage *at this time,* whateuer hee intended by it." The letter, dated London, March 19, 1659, is in *The Nicholas Papers,* ed. George F. Warner (London, 1920), pp. 195-96.
5. *Fasti*, II, col. 271.
6. Nethercot, *Abraham Cowley,* pp. 301-05, reprints the grant. The details of the years 1659-61 are admirably summarized in the biography, and I am indebted to Nethercot's account.
7. See Cowley's letter of May 13, 1667, to his friend John Evelyn (*Diary and Correspondence of John Evelyn,* ed. William Bray [London, 1854], III, 195-96): "I am ashamed of the rudeness I have committed in deferring so long my humble thanks for your obliging letter. . . . My laziness in finishing the copy of verses upon the Royal Society, for which I was engaged before by Mr. Sprat's desire, and encouraged since by you, was the cause of this delay, having designed to send it to you enclosed in my letter: but I am told now that the History is almost quite printed, and will be published so

soon, that it were impertinent labour to write out that which you will so suddenly see in a better manner, and in the company of better things. I could not comprehend in many of those excellent hints which you were pleased to give me, nor descend to the praises of particular persons, because those things afford too much matter for one copy of verse, and enough for a poem, or the History itself; some part of which I have seen, and think you will be very well satisfied with it."

8. Thomas Sprat, *A History of the Royal Society* (London, 1667), p. 59. "Sprat's account of the manner in which the Society originated . . . along with his implication that Cowley's *Proposition for the Advancement of Natural [sic] Philosophy* played an important part in its creation, have long been known to be inaccurate" (Jackson I. Cope and Harold Whitmore Jones, eds., *History of the Royal Society* [St. Louis, 1958], Appendix A, p. 65).

9. *Works*, I, 448-49.

10. *Ibid.*, pp. 451-52.

11. *Ibid.*, pp. 452-53.

12. See Nethercot, *Abraham Cowley*, pp. 413-29.

13. John Downes, *Roscius Anglicanus*, ed. Montague Summers (London, n.d.), p. 25.

14. John Dennis, "A Large Account of the Taste in Poetry," *Critical Essays of the XVIIIth Century*, ed. Willard H. Durham (New Haven, 1915), p. 131.

15. Downes, *Roscius Anglicanus*, p. 25.

16. Dennis, "A Large Account," pp. 131-32.

17. *Works*, I, 436-37; the lines are from *"The Complaint."*

18. *Ibid.*, pp. 411-12.

19. Readers may follow all the details of dating in A. H. Nethercot, "Abraham Cowley's Essays," *Journal of English and Germanic Philology*, XXIX (1930), 115-16, note 10.

20. "Account," II, 138.

21. "I thought," Cowley wrote in *"The Dangers of an Honest man in much Company,"* "when I went first to dwell in the Country, that without doubt I should have met there with the simplicity of the old Poetical Golden Age: I thought to have found no Inhabitants there, but such as the Shepherds of Sir. *Phil. Sydney in Arcadia,* or of *Monsieur d'Urfe* upon the Banks of *Lignon*: and began to consider with my self, which way I might recommend no less to Posterity the Happiness and Innocence of the Men of *Chertsea;* but to confess the truth, I perceived quickly, by infallible demonstrations, that I was still in Old *England,* and not in Arcadia, or La Forest" (*Works,* II, 446-47).

22. See Elbert N. S. Thompson, "The Seventeenth-Century Essay,"

University of Iowa Humanistic Studies, III (1926); W. L. Mac-
Donald, "Beginnings of the English Essay," *University of Toronto
Studies, Philological Series* No. 3 (1914), 1-122; and Walton, *Meta-
physical to Augustan,* pp. 94-120.

23. *The Letters of Charles Lamb, to which are added those of
his sister, Mary Lamb,* ed. E. V. Lucas (New Haven, 1935), I, 85.
The letter is dated January 10, 1797.

24. "Cowley," I, 64.

25. *"Of Obscurity," Works,* II, 399.

26. The edition of Cowley's essays by J. Rawson Lumby, rev.
Arthur Tilley (Cambridge, Eng., 1923), gives the conjectural order
of composition as follows: (1) *"Of Agriculture,"* (2) *"Of Liberty,"*
(3) *"Of Avarice,"* (4) *"The danger of Procrastination,"* (5) *"Of Soli-
tude,"* (6) *"Of Greatness,"* (7) *"The dangers of an Honest man in
much Company,"* (8) *"The shortness of Life and uncertainty of
Riches,"* (9) *"The Garden,"* (10) *"Of Obscurity,"* (11) *"Of My self"*
(p. xxiii).

27. *Works,* II, 403.

28. *Ibid.,* p. 405.

29. *Ibid.,* pp. 407-8.

30. *Ibid.,* p. 411.

31. Cowley must have known that, had he given us a complete
translation of the epode, its conclusion would have seriously undercut
the praise of country life which precedes it. At the conclusion we
discover that the speaker is Afius, a notorious usurer, himself ponder-
ing the values of rural retirement—after having bled his customers
of their livelihoods. Cowley omits the final ten lines of the epode
in order to present versions of poems by Vergil and Horace which
would complement one another. His readers, however, must have
recognized what he omitted from the epode.

32. The suggestion is S. Palmer Bovie's, made in the notes to his
superb translation of the *Satires* (Chicago, 1959), p. 82.

33. *Works,* II, 416.

34. *Ibid.,* p. 415.

35. *Ibid.*

36. *Metaphysical to Augustan,* p. 115.

37. *Works,* II, 418.

38. *Ibid.,* p. 420. Lest we think, however, that Cowley's life was
a rural idyll at Chertsey, we have his letter (one of those not
destroyed) to his friend Sprat, written from Chertsey on May 21,
1665: "The first night that I came hither I caught so great a cold,
with a defluxion of rheum, as made me keep my chamber ten days.
And, two after, had such a bruise on my ribs with a fall, that I am
yet unable to move or turn myself in my bed. This is my personal

fortune here to begin with. And, besides, I can get no money from my tenants and have my meadows eaten up every night by cattle put in by my neighbors. What this signifies, or may come to in time, God knows; if it be ominous, it can end in nothing less than hanging. Another misfortune has been, and stranger than all the rest, that you have broke your word with me, and failed to come, even though you told Mr. Bois that you would. This is what they call *Monstri simile*. I do hope to recover my late hurt so farre within five or six days (though it be uncertain yet where I shall ever recover it) as to walk about again. And then, methinks, you and I and *the Dean* might be very merry upon St. Anne's Hill. You might very conveniently come hither the way of Hampton Town, lying there one night. I write this in pain and can say no more. Verbum Sapienti." (As cited in Johnson, "Cowley," I, 16-17).

39. "Account," II, 139.

40. *Works*, II, 455-56.

41. *Ibid.*, pp. 457-58.

42. *Ibid.*, I, 6.

43. *Ibid.*, p. 8.

44. *Ibid.*

45. (London, 1667), p. 59.

46. *Works*, II, 256.

47. Cowley probably remembered his own difficulties in language study: "My Masters could never prevail on me, by any perswasions or encouragements, to learn without Book the common rules of Grammar, in which they dispensed with me alone, because they found I made a shift to do the usual exercises out of my own reading and observation" (*"Of My self," ibid.*, p. 456).

48. John Sargeaunt, *Annals of Westminster School* (London, 1898), p. 124.

49. See H. R. Mead, "Two Issues of Cowley's 'Vision,'" *Papers of the Bibliographical Society of America*, XLV (1951), 77-81.

50. "Advertisements," *Works*, II, 493. Cowley is probably the author.

51. See Isaiah XIII on the "Burdens of Babylon." The term, a common biblical one, means lot or fate; and Cowley's use of it here defines the voice he assumes for the tract.

52. *Cowley: Essays and Other Prose Writings* (London, 1915), p. 263.

53. *Works*, II, 345-46.

54. *Ibid.*, pp. 347-48.

55. *Ibid.*, p. 369.

56. *Ibid.*, p. 371. C. H. Firth's article "Cromwelliana," *Notes and Queries*, Series IX, VII (1901), 481-82, notes that the story of

Cromwell's comments on Magna Carta appeared several times in 1659, that it is unlikely the Protector ever made them, and "it is pretty clear that the story was invented several years after the event by Cromwell's political opponents" (p. 482).

57. *Works,* II, 375.

58. *Ibid.,* p. 263.

59. *Ibid.,* p. 264.

60. *Ibid.,* pp. 265-66.

61. "Account," II, 142.

62. *Ibid.,* p. 143.

63. *Cowley's History of Plants,* ed. and trans. Nahum Tate *et al.* (London, 1795), pp. xx-xxi. The Latin poems are available only in Alexander Grosart's two-volume edition of *The Complete Works in Verse and Prose of Abraham Cowley* (Edinburgh, 1881).

64. Tate, *History of Plants,* p. xxi.

65. Hinman, *Abraham Cowley,* p. 273. Hinman's chapter on the history of plants (pp. 267-96) is an excellent discussion to which I am greatly indebted.

66. Tate, *History of Plants,* pp. 31-34; Grosart, *Works,* II, 149-50.

67. *Ibid.,* p. 41; *ibid.,* p. 154.

68. *Ibid.,* pp. 45-46; *ibid.,* p. 157.

69. *Ibid.,* p. 77; *ibid.,* p. 172.

70. *Ibid.,* pp. 94-95; *ibid.,* pp. 181-82.

71. *Ibid.,* pp. 128-29; *ibid.,* pp. 199-200.

72. Thomas Sprat, "Account," II, 136.

73. Tate, *History of Plants,* p. 165; Grosart, *Works,* II, 219.

Chapter Seven

1. John Dryden, "Progress of Satire," *Essays,* II, 76.

2. "*Of Agriculture,*" *Works,* I, 404.

3. See the two articles by Joseph A. Mazzeo, "A Critique of Some Modern Theories of Metaphysical Poetry," *Modern Philology,* L (1952), 88-96; "Metaphysical Poetry and the Poetic of Correspondence," *Journal of the History of Ideas,* XIV (1953), 221-34. See also L. C. Knights, "On the Social Background of Metaphysical Poetry," *Scrutiny,* XIII (1945), 37-53; and Robin Skelton, "The Poetry of John Donne," *Elizabethan Poetry, Stratford-Upon-Avon Studies* No. 2 (London, 1960), 203-20.

4. "The Metaphysical Poets," *Selected Essays* (New York, 1950), p. 245.

5. "The Garden," *Works,* II, 427.

6. The comment is dated October 23, 1773 ("The Journal of a Tour to the Hebrides with Samuel Johnson, L.L.D.," *The Life of Johnson,* ed. G. Birkbeck Hill, rev. L. F. Powell [London, 1934-50], V, 345).

Selected Bibliography

For a complete bibliography of the English writings, the reader may consult Geoffrey Walton's Cambridge University doctoral dissertation, "The English Writings of Abraham Cowley" (1940).

PRIMARY SOURCES

COWLEY, ABRAHAM. *The Mistresse or Seuerall Copies of Love Verses.* London: Humphrey Moseley, 1647.

————. *Poems: Viz. I. Miscellanies, II. The Mistress, or, Love Verses, III. Pindarique Odes, and IV. Davideis, or, a Sacred Poem of the Troubles of David.* London: Humphrey Moseley, 1656.

————. *The Works of Mr. Abraham Cowley.* London: Henry Herringman, 1668.

————. *Abrahami Couleij Angli, Poemata Latina.* Londini, J. Martyn, 1668.

————. *Works.* London: Henry Herringman, 1674 [a fourth edition].

————. *Works.* London: Henry Herringman, 1693 [an eighth edition].

————. *Works.* London: H. Herringman, 1700 [a ninth edition].

————. *Select Works in Verse and Prose,* ed. Richard Hurd. 2 vols. London: T. Cadell, 1772 [a third edition in 1777].

————. *Cowley's History of Plants, a poem in six books. . . .* Trans. Nahum Tate *et al.* London: J. Smeeton, 1795.

————. *The Complete Works in Verse and Prose of Abraham Cowley. Now for the First Time Collected and Edited: with Memorial-Introduction and Notes and Illustrations, Portraits, Etc.,* ed. Alexander Grosart. 2 vols. Edinburgh: The Chertsey Worthies Library, 1881. A valuable edition, still the only complete collection. Grosart's long prose introduction is a masterpiece of nineteenth-century adulation.

————. *The English Writings of Abraham Cowley: Poems.* Ed. A. R. Waller. Cambridge, England: Cambridge University Press, 1905. The standard edition; presently out of print. Records textual variants, but has no critical notes.

————. *Essays, Plays and Sundry Verses.* Ed. A. R. Waller. Cambridge, England: Cambridge University Press, 1906. Standard edition; without critical notes.

————. *The Essays and Other Prose Writings.* Ed. A. B. Gough. Oxford: Oxford University Press, 1915. Fine separate edition; complete with careful biographical and critical notes.

————. *Cowley's Essays.* Ed. J. Rawson Lumby; rev. Arthur Tilley. Cambridge University Press, 1923. Helpful alternative edition to that of A. R. Gough.

————. *The Mistress with other Select Poems of Abraham Cowley.* Ed. John Sparrow. London: The Nonesuch Press, 1926. Handsome edition for the Nonesuch Press; includes biographical material in the introduction.

————. *Abraham Cowley: Poetry and Prose, with Thomas Sprat's Life. . . .* Ed. L. C. Martin. Oxford: The Clarendon Press, 1949. Only recent anthology of Cowley's work; preceded by a rich selection of historical commentary from Dryden to Grierson.

————. *Abraham Cowley: Selected Poetry and Prose.* Ed. James G. Taaffe. New York: Appleton-Century-Crofts, 1970. A new edition in the Crofts Classics.

SECONDARY SOURCES

Anon. *The True Effigies of the Monster of Malmesbury, or Thomas Hobbes in His Proper Colours.* London: n.p., 1680. A two-part attack—preface and lampoon—the latter by a "Lover of Truth and Virtue"—upon Hobbes. The poem burlesques Cowley's commendatory ode, juxtaposing those stanzas with appropriate "answers."

ARBER, EDWARD (ed.). *A Transcript of the Registers of the Company of Stationers of London.* 4 vols., plus index, Oxford: The Clarendon Press, 1875-94. Chronological listing of those books registered with the guild for publication.

BARNES, JOSHUA (ed.). *Anacreon Teius Poeta Lyricus, Summa Cura et Diligentia ad Fidem Etiam, Vet. Ms. Vatacani.* Cantabrigiae: Edmundi Jeffrey, 1705. Important early eighteenth-century edition of Anacreon; its prose commentary is the source for the comment that Cowley had once been in love and was too shy to declare himself.

BUSH, DOUGLAS. *Mythology and the Renaissance Tradition in English Poetry.* New rev. ed. New York: W. W. Norton, 1963. Survey of Classical mythology and its influence on sixteenth- and seventeenth-century poetry; valuable appendix provides "a chronological conspectus of mythological poems."

————. *English Literature in the Earlier Seventeenth Century.* 2nd ed. Oxford: The Clarendon Press, 1962. Standard volume in the Oxford series of literary histories; it examines popular literature, the prose and poetry from Jonson and Donne, concluding with Milton. Valuable chronologies and bibliographies.

CHALMERS, ALEXANDER (ed.). *The Works of the English Poets.* . . . 21 vols. London: J. Johnson, 1810. Valuable anthology of little-known poets.

COHANE, J. J. "Cowley and Yeats." *Times Literary Supplement,* May 10, 1957, p. 289. A comment on the possibility that the stanzaic form of Cowley's "On the Death of Mr. William Harvey" was appropriated by Yeats in several poems.

CRANE, WILLIAM G. *Wit and Rhetoric in the Renaissance.* New York: Columbia University Press, 1937. Historical study of both concepts—and of their relationship.

CRASHAW, RICHARD. *The Poems, English Latin and Greek of Richard Crashaw.* Ed. L. C. Martin. Oxford: The Clarendon Press, 1927. Standard edition; a revision was issued in 1957.

DAVENANT, WILLIAM. "A Discourse upon Gondibert, An Heroick Poem." *Critical Essays of the Seventeenth Century.* Vol. II. Ed. J. E. Spingarn. 3 vols. Bloomington: Indiana University Press, 1957. The essay, first published in Paris in 1650 and addressed to Hobbes, surveys epic poetry from Homer to Spenser, resolves upon the significance of the religious epic, justifies stanzaic form, etc. It is an important critical document for seventeenth-century discussions of taste and imagery.

DENNIS, JOHN. "A Large Account of the Taste in Poetry." *Critical Essays of the XVIIIth Century.* Ed. Willard H. Durham. New Haven: Yale University Press, 1915. Originally the preface to Dennis's version of *The Merry Wives of Windsor* (1702), the essay discusses the generally lower standards of audience which prevail in his time than those in the time of Charles II; it contains a scathing denunciation of Cibber and others.

DOWNES, JOHN. *Roscius Anglicanus.* Ed. Montague Summers. London: The Fortune Press, 1928. In spite of errors in chronology and fact, this historical review of the stage from 1660 to 1706 provides valuable information on casts and the popularity and frequency of performance.

DRYDEN, JOHN. "The Preface to Ovid's Epistles. . . ." *Of Dramatic Poesy and Other Critical Essays.* Vol. II. Ed. George Watson. 2 vols. London: J. M. Dent & Sons, 1962. Dryden's first important essay on translation (1680), cited by Johnson as partially responsible for "breaking the shackles of verbal interpretation, which must forever debar it from elegance."

————. "A Discourse Concerning the Original and Progress of Satire." *Of Dramatic Poesy and Other Critical Essays.* Vol. II. Ed. George Watson. 2 vols. London: J. M. Dent & Sons, 1962. Dedicated to the Eugenius of *Of Dramatic Poesy* (Charles, Earl

of Dorset), the preface is a significant attempt to survey a
literary form; it discusses Percius, Horace, and Juvenal, and
contains the famous analogy between the satirist and Jack Ketch
the executioner.

ELIOT, T. S. "The Metaphysical Poets," in *Selected Essays*. New
York: Harcourt, Brace, 1950. Famous review of Grierson's an-
thology (1921). Eliot's essay discusses the extended comparison,
the telescoping image, the seventeenth-century "dissociation of
sensibility."

ELLEDGE, SCOTT. "Cowley's Ode 'Of Wit' and Longinus on the Sub-
lime: A Study of One Definition of the Word 'Wit.' " *Modern
Language Quarterly*, IX (1948), 185-98. Numerous parallels
between Cowley's ode and Longinus's work; "wit" associated
in the seventeenth century with the sublime, with what was
thought of as "high" in poetry.

ELYS, EDMUND. *An Exclamation to All those that Love the Lord Jesus
in Sincerity, Against an Apology Written by an Ingenious Person,
For Mr. Cowley's Lascivious and Profane Verses*. London: n.p.,
1670. Spiteful and sanctimonious attack on the love verses of
The Mistress.

FIRTH, C. H. "Abraham Cowley at the Restoration." *The Academy*,
MCXVIII (1893), 296. Epistolary exchange of 1659 and 1660
between Cowley and Ormond over the former's status with
Charles. The letters are from the Carte Mss. in the Bodleian.

————. "Cromwelliana." *Notes and Queries*, Series IX, VII (1901),
481-82. Convincing argument to disprove the rumors that Crom-
well had threatened to suspend or revoke the Magna Carta.

GENEST, JOHN. *Some Account of the English Stage*. 10 vols. Bath:
H. E. Carrington, 1832. Chronological survey of plays and casts
from 1660 to 1830.

GOLDSTEIN, HARVEY D. "Cowley and the Pindarick Madness." Un-
published doctoral dissertation, Northwestern, 1960. Focusing on
the Pindarics, because they reveal "the major aesthetic conflicts
of the mid-seventeenth century," Goldstein sees Cowley's esthetic
as both Augustan and metaphysical.

GOSSE, EDMUND. *Seventeenth Century Studies: A Contribution to the
History of English Poetry*. London: K. Paul, Trench & Co., 1883.
Group of essays "to do for the rank and file of seventeenth
century literature what modern criticism has done . . . for
Shakespeare, Milton, and Dryden," with consideration of Lodge,
Webster, Rowlands, Otway *et al*.

GREG, W. W. *Pastoral Poetry and Pastoral Drama*. London: A. H.
Bullen, 1906. Fine history, with bibliography, emphasizing pre-
Restoration drama.

HINMAN, ROBERT. *Abraham Cowley's World of Order.* Cambridge,
Mass.: Harvard University Press, 1960. Major assessment of the
relationship between science and literature in the seventeenth
century with Cowley as the focal point.

HOBBES, THOMAS. "The Answer of Mr. Hobbes to Sr. Will. Davenant's
Preface Before *Gondibert.*" *Critical Essays of the Seventeenth
Century.* Vol. II. Ed. J. E. Spingarn. 3 vols. Bloomington: Indiana
University Press, 1957. The famous definition of wit and judg-
ment appears in this important statement of seventeenth-century
esthetic theory.

HORACE (Quintus Horatius Flaccus). *The Odes and Epodes of Horace.*
Trans. Joseph P. Clancy. Chicago: University of Chicago Press,
1960. Excellent translation in paperback intended "primarily for
readers with little or no Latin."

JOHNSON, SAMUEL. "Cowley." *Lives of the English Poets.* Vol. I. Ed.
G. Birkbeck Hill. 3 vols. Oxford: The Clarendon Press, 1905.
The first, and Johnson thought the best, of his lives of the poets.
An assessment of Cowley's career and of Metaphysical poetry.

KERMODE, FRANK. "The Date of Cowley's *Davideis.*" *Review of Eng-
lish Studies,* XXV (1949), 154-58. Argues convincingly to date
the epic's composition from 1651 or 1652 to 1654.

KNIGHTS, L. C. "On the Social Background of Metaphysical Poetry."
Scrutiny, XIII (1945), 37-53. "An attempt to work out from
literature—from Metaphysical poetry—to "the life of time" in the
early seventeenth century."

LOISEAU, JEAN. *Abraham Cowley, sa Vie, son Oeuvre.* Paris: Henri
Didier, 1931. Only definitive study of Cowley's poetics; has also
a complete and accurate biography.

————. *Abraham Cowley's Reputation in England.* Paris: Henri
Didier, 1931. Careful review of the course of Cowley's popularity,
with many examples of contemporary opinion.

MCBRYDE, JOHN L. JR. "A Study of Cowley's *Davideis.*" *Journal of
English and Germanic Philology,* II (1900), 454-527; III (1901),
24-35. First extensive study of sources and analogues, including
statistical notes on metrics and stanzaic forms. McBryde con-
cludes that Cowley's verse became more regular and correct
as he matured.

MACDONALD, W. L. "Beginnings of the English Essay." *University of
Toronto Studies, Philological Series.* No. 3. Toronto: University
of Toronto Press, 1914. Convenient history, including definitions
of the term "essay," and a discussion of its prototypes and allied
forms.

MAZZEO, JOSEPH ANTHONY. "A Critique of Some Modern Theories
of Metaphysical Poetry." *Modern Philology,* L (1952), 88-96.

Fine article on poetics; concludes that "the qualities of the metaphysical image are a function of the *manner* in which the analogues are related."

——. "Metaphysical Poetry and the Poetry of Correspondence." *Journal of the History of Ideas,* XIV (1953), 221-34. Concentrating on Continental views of *concettismo* and *acutezze,* shows that the conceit and metaphor are the law by which creation was effected.

MEAD, H. R. "Two Issues of Cowley's 'Vision.'" *Papers of the Bibliographical Society of America,* XLV (1951), 77-81. Notes an appearance of an early (1660) version of Cowley's essay on Cromwell.

NATHANSON, LEONARD. "The Context of Dryden's Criticism of Donne's and Cowley's Love Poetry." *Notes and Queries,* CCII (1956), 56-59.

NETHERCOT, ARTHUR H. "The Relation of Cowley's 'Pindarics' to Pindar's Odes." *Modern Philology,* XIX (1921), 107-9. Cowley, Nethercot argues, did know his Pindar well.

——. "Abraham Cowley as Dramatist." *Review of English Studies,* IV (1928), 1-24. Survey of the drama, its sources, dates, and popularity.

——. "Abraham Cowley's Essays." *Journal of English and Germanic Philology,* XXIX (1930), 114-30. Discussion of the essays, form, and content.

——. *Abraham Cowley: The Muse's Hannibal.* Oxford: Oxford University Press, 1931. The standard English biography.

NOLL, LOU BAKER. "Abraham Cowley's Lyric Achievement." Unpublished doctoral dissertation, Colorado, 1959. Concentrates on the poetical voices or masks of Abraham Cowley; a suggestion of "new ways for the reader to approach the lyrical I-speaking works of Cowley."

OSBORNE, DOROTHY. *The Letters of Dorothy Osborne to William Temple.* Ed. G. C. Moore Smith. Oxford: The Clarendon Press, 1928. The standard edition of the letters of the "matchless Orinda," who, in several letters, comments on Cowley.

RAJAN, B. *Paradise Lost and the Seventeenth-Century Reader.* 2nd ed. London: Chatto and Windus, 1962. An argument that *Paradise Lost* must be read in an historical context, for those "contemporary" attitudes must be part of what a reader brings to the poem if he is to understand Milton.

RAWLINSON, DAVID. "Cowley and the Current Status of Metaphysical Poetry." *Essays in Criticism,* XIII (1963), 323-40. Review of the unsympathetic attitude toward Cowley, and an attempt to show where his strength lies (especially in the essays).

SAINTSBURY, GEORGE (ed.). *Minor Poets of the Caroline Period.* 3 vols. Oxford: The Clarendon Press, 1905-21. Classic anthology representing minor figures in depth.

SARGEAUNT, JOHN. *Annals of Westminster School.* London: Methuen & Co., 1968. A "biography" of the famous public school.

SHAFER, ROBERT. *The English Ode to 1660.* Princeton: Princeton University Press, 1918. Chronological history of the ode, its Classical prototypes, Pindaric modifications, the odes of Jonson and Cowley.

SHUSTER, GEORGE N. *The English Ode from Milton to Keats.* New York: Columbia University Press, 1940. Detailed history of the form from Milton through the Romantics with an excellent opening chapter on the genre. A well-documented compliment to Shafer's history.

SPARROW, JOHN. "The Text of Cowley's *Mistress.*" *Review of English Studies,* III (1927), 22-27. Important discussion of variant texts of the love poems.

SPENCE, JOSEPH. *Anecdotes, Observations, and Characters, of Books and Men, Collected from the Conversations of Mr. Pope, and other Eminent Persons of his Time.* Ed. Samuel W. Singer. London: J. Murry, 1820. Collection of miscellaneous, often erroneous, comments.

SPRAT, THOMAS. *A History of the Royal Society.* London: J. Martyn, 1667. The famous account of the society's founding and some of its experiments.

————. *A History of the Royal Society.* Ed. Jackson I. Cope and Harold Whitmore Jones. St. Louis: Washington University Press, 1958. Our modern edition of Sprat; fine notes, well annotated.

————. "An Account of the Life and Writings of Mr. Abraham Cowley. . . ." *Critical Essays of the Seventeenth Century.* Vol. II. Ed. J. E. Spingarn. 3 vols. Bloomington: Indiana University Press, 1957. The first life of Cowley; a bit of adulatory hero worship.

THOMPSON, E. N. S. "The Seventeenth-Century Essay." *University of Iowa Humanistic Studies.* Vol. III. Iowa City: University of Iowa, 1926. History of the essay as genre, its sources and various allied forms.

WALTON, GEOFFREY. *From Metaphysical to Augustan.* London: Bowes and Bowes, 1955. Sensitive, careful discussion of the transition, with emphasis on Cowley, from one style to another.

WARREN, AUSTIN. *Richard Crashaw: A Study in Baroque Sensibility.* University, La.: The Louisiana State University Press, 1939. The standard study of Crashaw; indispensable.

WEDGWOOD, CECILY. *Seventeenth-Century English Literature.* New

York: Oxford University Press, 1961. Illuminating, informal discussion of the literature; one of the best short studies.

WESLEY, SAMUEL. *The Preface . . . Being an Essay on Heroick Poetry. The Augustan Reprint Society, Second Series*. Ann Arbor: University of Michigan Press, 1947. The father of the great religious leader defends the biblical and Christian epic.

WILLIAMSON, GEORGE. *The Donne Tradition: A Study in English Poetry from Donne to the Death of Cowley*. Cambridge, Mass.: Harvard University Press, 1930. Outdated, but still a valuable exercise in the appraisal of the followers of Donne.

WOOD, ANTHONY À. *Fasti Oxonienses*. 2 vols. London: J. Tonson *et al.*, 1721. A frequently biased and incorrect work; nonetheless, valuable as a record of Oxford alumni, their families, friends, and accomplishments.

Index

(The works of Cowley are listed under his name)

Addison, Joseph, 101, 122
Alexander, 18
Anacreon, 43-46, 49
Augustine, St., 86
a Wood, Anthony, 96

Bacon, Francis, 96-97, 101, 102, 108, 109
Barnes, Joshua, 49
Bellamy, Daniel, 27
Betterton, Thomas, 98
Betterton, Mrs., 98
Boswell, James, 123
Boyle, Robert, 35, 69, 101, 108
Broghill (Roger Boyle, 1st Earl of Orrery), 99
Brutus, 68-69
Buckingham, Duchess of, 20-21
Bush, Douglas, 76-77

Caesar, Julius, 68
Cartwright, Thomas, 22
Cary, Lucius, 34, 37
Cervius, 104
Charles I, 19-20, 23, 25, 68, 93, 95-96, 98
Charles II, 30, 111-12, 117, 119-20
Cicero, 18, 109
Clarendon, Earl of, 101
Cleveland, John, 58, 122
Clifford, Martin, 78
Coleridge, Samuel, 101
Collins, William, 122
Comber, Dr., 29-30
Cowley, Abraham: at Westminster, 13, 25; graduation from Westminster, 19; published first poems, *Poetical Blossoms*, 13; entered Trinity College, 19; on Isle of

Jersey, 60, 79; imprisonment, 68, 71, 108; in France, 79, 110; return of Trinity fellowship by Charles II, 96; received some land in Kent from Queen Henrietta Maria for services rendered her during exile, 96; retirement to Kent, 99

WORKS:

"*Account, The*," 46
"*Against Fruition*," 51
"*Age*," 45
"*Anacreontics*," 34, 43-46
"*Answer to an Invitation to Cambridge, An*," 25
"*Beatus ille qui procure...*," (translation of Horace), 104
"*Brutus*," 68
"*Called Inconstant*," 52
"*Chronicle, The*," 46
"*Constantia and Philetus*," 13-17, 20
"*Country Mouse, The*," (translation of Horace), 104-5
"*Cutter of Coleman Street*," Preface to, 107, 112-13
"*Danger of Procrastination, The*," 100
Davideis, 41, 73, 75-94, 99, 114-15, 122, 123-24; character, 83-94; allegory, 89, 92; female characters, 84-85; versification, 85
"*Destinie*," 70-71
"*Discovery, The*," 51
Discourse by way of Vision, A, 107

153